Lord, Teach Us to Pray

Other books by Fulton J. Sheen
from Sophia Institute Press:

The Cries of Jesus from the Cross
A Fulton Sheen Anthology

Fulton Sheen's Wartime Prayer Book

God's World and Our Place in It

Victory over Vice

Archbishop Fulton J. Sheen

LORD, TEACH US TO PRAY

A FULTON SHEEN ANTHOLOGY

Compiled by Al Smith

SOPHIA INSTITUTE PRESS

Manchester, New Hampshire

Sophia Institute Press
Box 5284, Manchester, NH 03108
1-800-888-9344

www.SophiaInstitute.com

Sophia Institute Press® is a registered trademark of Sophia Institute.

Library of Congress Cataloging-in-Publication Data

Library of Congress cataloging-in-publication data has been applied for.

ISBN 978-1-64413-083-4

First printing

JMJ

To St. Joseph,
spouse of the Blessed Virgin Mary
and guardian of the Redeemer:

In humble petition to St. Joseph, who taught Jesus
how to pray, that he, in like manner,
will assist and guide us in our own prayer lives.

As St. Joseph adored the Christ Child with great
awe and profound reverence during his life, may we,
too, gaze upon the Lord in the Most Blessed Sacrament
with that same adoration and devotion.

Lord, teach us to pray.
—Luke 11:1

Contents

Introduction xi

1. The Seven Last Words 3

   Introduction 5

   First Word: Our Father, Who Art in Heaven 7

   Second Word: Hallowed Be Thy Name 9

   Third Word: Thy Kingdom Come 11

   Fourth Word: Thy Will Be Done on Earth as It Is in Heaven. 13

   Fifth Word: Give Us This Day Our Daily Bread. 17

   Sixth Word: Forgive Us Our Trespasses as We Forgive
   Those Who Trespass against Us 19

   Seventh Word: Deliver Us from Evil 21

2. Calvary and the Mass: A Missal Companion 23

   Prologue 25

   The Confiteor 33

   The Offertory. 39

   The Sanctus 45

   The Consecration 51

The Communion 57

The Ite, Missa Est. 63

The Last Gospel 69

3. The Holy Hour: Meditations and Reflections 77

"Could You Not Watch One Hour with Me?" 79

First Meditation: The Incarnation of Our Lord
and Savior, Jesus Christ 99

Second Meditation: How Christ Lives in Us Today 105

Third Meditation: How That Divine Life Is Lost
and Our Final End 113

Fourth Meditation: The Duty of Self-Denial 121

Fifth Meditation: Giving Glory to God in the World 129

Sixth Meditation: The Eucharist, the Need of Our Heart. 139

Seventh Meditation: Our Blessed Mother 147

4. The Stations of the Cross 159

5. Thoughts for Meditation 163

Thoughts on Faith and Belief 165

Thoughts on the Spiritual Battle 169

Thoughts on Prayer and Sacrifice 175

Thoughts on Looking into My Soul 185

Thoughts on Encouragement. 193

Thoughts on the Eucharist 199

Thoughts on the Blessed Mother 211

6. Prayers of Meditation and Petition 217

　Christ to a Faithful Soul 217

　Prayer to Follow the Example of Jesus Christ 218

　Prayer against Evil Thoughts. 218

　Prayer for the Enlightening of the Mind. 219

　Prayer for Charity and Tolerance 220

　A Universal Prayer 221

　Prayer of St. Ignatius 223

　A Prayer of the Church under Grievous Persecutions 223

　A Prayer of a Sinner, Trusting in the Mercies of God 224

　Prayer before a Crucifix 224

　An Exhortation to the Praise and Service of God 224

　An Exhortation to Despise This World and the Short Prosperity
　of the Wicked and to Trust in Providence. 226

　"To Our Lady". 227

Acknowledgments 229

About the Author: Fulton J. Sheen. 231

Fulton J. Sheen Works Used in This Book. 233

Introduction

*And it came to pass, that as He was in a certain place pray-
ing. When He ceased, one of His disciples said to Him: "Lord,
teach us to pray, as John also taught his disciples."*

—Luke 11:1

It was over two thousand years ago that the disciples of Jesus asked Him
to teach them to pray. The desire both to know how to pray and to have
a prayer life that is satisfying is one that continues to stir in hearts today.

Our Lord lovingly fulfilled the disciples' request when He taught them
to pray the Our Father (Luke 11:1–4). By His example, He showed them
the necessity of going to a quiet place to pray, to receive guidance and
spiritual nourishment (Mark 1:35; Luke 5:16; Matt. 14:23).

While addressing the crowd gathered on the mount, Jesus was likewise
reminding the disciples, "When you pray, go into your room and shut
the door and pray to your Father who is in secret; and your Father who
sees in secret will reward you" (Matt. 6:6).

Archbishop Fulton J. Sheen received this same request that was made
of Our Lord: teach us to pray. His students, his parishioners, and his
worldwide audience would ask him about ways to pray and about his
favorite prayers.

With this in mind, Sheen was keen to encourage people to make prayer a daily, holy habit. To Catholics, he would specifically recommend attending Holy Mass daily whenever possible, to set aside time to pray a Holy Hour, and to pray the Way of the Cross in union with Our Lord's Passion.

Archbishop Fulton J. Sheen was known to have often said: "I do not want my life to be mine. I want it to be Christ's." He had cultivated an intimate prayer life with Christ, and he wanted to share it with everyone.

Over the years, while hosting *The Catholic Hour* radio show, Sheen produced several little prayer books with the help of the National Council of Catholic Men. These prayer books were printed and distributed in the hundreds of thousands, and some are still in distribution. The themes of these prayer books have been incorporated into this anthology.

Here, Archbishop Sheen will take us on a journey of prayer, a mini-retreat highlighting the central events in the life of Christ: His Passion, His Death, His Resurrection, His sending of the Holy Spirit, and His coming again in glory.

Through Sheen's thoughtful meditations and reflections, the reader will be invited to follow Christ, to imitate Him, to learn from Him, to possess Him, and to be possessed by Him.

Each of the six chapters in this book has a unique theme, presented in that classic Sheen style, both deep and succinct: "The Our Father," "The Mass," "The Holy Hour," "Thoughts for Meditation," "The Way of the Cross," and "Prayers of Meditation and Petition."

On the topic of Our Father, we will begin with Sheen's Good Friday address of April 19, 1935. During this reflection, in order to help bring the reader into a deeper understanding of the Lord's Prayer, Sheen uses as a teaching tool the lens of the seven last words spoken by Our Lord from the Cross.

Employing once again the same lens of the seven last words, Archbishop Sheen sheds further light on the Holy Sacrifice of the Mass, which Our Lord instituted on Holy Thursday. Sheen's classic "Calvary and the Mass," penned in 1936, is included in the second chapter.

Introduction

In the third chapter, Archbishop Sheen presents his insights on the Holy Hour. The reader will find a number of moving meditations that will lend themselves to making a fruitful Holy Hour. Some might ask, "Why spend an hour a day in meditation?" to which Archbishop Sheen would respond, "Because we are living on the surface of our souls, knowing little either of God or our inner self. Our knowledge is mostly about things, not about destiny."

The fourth chapter contains a popular version of the Way of the Cross. It is hoped that these beautiful indulgenced prayers will enkindle a holy love for the Crucified Savior.

The final two chapters of this book are made up of holy reflections and prayers, eliciting "heart speaks to heart" moments. "Draw near to God, and He will draw near to you" (James 4:8).

In this book, Archbishop Sheen not only unpacks the central mysteries of the Catholic Faith but also, in his inimitable way, crystallizes what it is to have a meaningful relationship with God.

Everyone is called to prayer and relationship. It is my hope that in reading this volume, the reader will experience a sentiment similar to Archbishop Sheen's: "I do not want my life to be mine. I want it to be Christ's."

Lord, Teach Us to Pray

1

The Seven Last Words

Radio address delivered on The Catholic Hour
on Good Friday, April 19, 1935

Introduction

Our Lord is the only king who ever stumbled to His throne. But that was because He is God, and God reveals His Power through the weakness of a crucifixion and His wisdom through the foolishness of a cross.

Once on the heights of Calvary, where meet the crossroads of the three civilizations in whose name He is crucified, He is fittingly stripped of His garments. They belong to His time, to Judea, to Galilee, to a small province of Rome. Now, in order that He might not be localized by garments but universalized as Redeemer of the world, He permits Himself to be shorn of the last vestige of earthly things so as to be utterly and absolutely the poor man of the world.

What message will the King deliver from His unkingly throne? Last words are always important but particularly the last words of Him who gave His life for the redemption of many! It will be recalled that one day, the Apostles approached Him, saying: "Lord, teach us to pray." He answered their request by giving them the perfect prayer: the Our Father. Now the time comes for Him to say His own "Our Father." As there were seven petitions in the Our Father that He taught us, so there are seven petitions in His own last prayer. They are known as the Seven Last Words. We shall meditate conjointly on our Our Father and on His "Our Father."

Our Father, Who Art in Heaven

Father, forgive them for they know not what they do.

—Luke 23:34

The first petition of the Our Father that Our Lord taught us was the prayer of priestly intercession: "Our Father, who art in heaven." The first word from the Cross was the intercessory prayer of the perfect Priest: "Father, forgive them for they know not what they do."

The Priest whence all priesthood is derived once asked us to look up to our Father who is in heaven. Now He begs that same Father to blot out the sins of those who crucify Him and to forgive them, "for they know not what they do." He was finding an excuse for sins. He was telling His Father that we crucified Him only because of our ignorance. If we knew what we were doing, we would never have denied the Father in heaven. Salvation is possible only because of our ignorance of how good God the Father is to send His only-begotten Son into the world that we might have life in His name.

When our enemies crucify us, we say: "They should have known better." When we crucified Him, He said: "Forgive them, for they know not what they do." We love those who love us and honor those who flatter us; He loved those who hated Him and forgave even the hands that drove the nails. He loves not only the lovable, as we do; He also loves the hateful, which we are. That is why there is hope for us! Our Father, who art in heaven, forgive us, for we know not what we do."

Hallowed Be Thy Name

Amen, I say to thee, this day thou shalt be with me in paradise.

—Luke 23:43

God's name is hallowed by the recognition of His power and glory. The thief recognized God's power despite His powerlessness, and God's glory despite His defeat.

Picture two scenes as this second word is being spoken. On opposite sides of Zion, there were men hanging on trees. On one side of the hill, Judas was hanging from a tree; on the opposite side hung Our Lord between two thieves. Note the difference in attitude of Judas and the thief on the right. Both were thieves. But there was this difference. Judas thought God's glory was purely external, manifested by earthly pomp and circumstance. Hence, when he saw Our Lord go down in defeat, he sold Him for thirty pieces of silver. The thief on the left of Our Lord was like Judas. He, too, felt that the only power worth having was the power of saving him from pain. Hence, he cried in agony: "Save thyself and us" (Luke 23:39). In other words, do something external. But the thief on the right moved his pain-racked head toward Our Lord, saw Him divested of every robe of royalty, and denuded of every badge of kingship. And yet he perceived the gold beneath the dust, and the kingdom through a cloud, and power to save a soul beneath the weakness of

9

a drained body: "Lord, remember me when Thou shalt come into Thy Kingdom" (Luke 23:42).

Our Blessed Savior was so pleased to find His name hallowed amid blasphemy, and His blessing recognized amid curses, that He granted the humble prayer of the thief: "Amen, I say to thee, this day thou shalt be with me in paradise."

The world is full of Judases who think the name of God is hallowed only by worldly pomp and splendor. They forget that the kingdom of God is internal and "cometh not by observation" (see Luke 17:20) and that the Church, which is the Mystical Christ, manifests her greatest strength in the forgiveness of sins.

The world asks: "How can man forgive sin?" It might just as well ask how a man whose kingdom is no wider than a beam of wood could promise the kingdom of heaven to a thief.

The forgiveness of sin is a greater manifestation of the power of God than the creation of the world. Creation makes something out of nothing. Forgiveness puts something into nothing. But the forgiveness that opens paradise is obtained as the thief obtained his, namely, by asking for it. Pardon, like all gifts of God, is conditioned. The latch on the door of divine forgiveness is on the inside of our souls—on our side, not on God's side. "Behold, I stand at the door and knock" (see Rev. 3:20). He knocks! He does not force down the door. That would destroy human freedom. He knocks to be admitted; we alone have the power to unlatch the door to invite Him in, that He may sup with us and we with Him. Christ's greatest sorrow is to be denied admittance. "You will not come to me" (John 5:40). His greatest joy is to be welcomed even by sinners, for "there is more joy in heaven for one sinner doing penance than for ninety-nine just who need not penance" (Luke 15:7). There is no power as strong as the uplifted hand of an absolving priest; there is no joy like the return of a prodigal; there is no peace like the peace of sin forgiven. There is no hope like the hope the thief gives us: paradise may still be stolen.

Thy Kingdom Come

Woman, behold thy son.

—John 19:26

When Our Lord taught us the "Our Father" He made the third petition a prayer that God's kingdom, which is the kingdom of saints, might come. Now, in His own last prayer, He addresses the saintliest of creatures: Mary, His mother, and John, the beloved disciple. He was dying on the Cross for no other reason than to make us saints—and to be a saint means to be fixed in goodness. The saintliest creature God ever made was the Mother of His Divine Son, for she was not only "full of grace" but a co-Redeemer with her Son, now suspended above her head. When Our Lord looked down to her and commended her to us in the person of John, saying: "Behold thy mother," He was equivalently telling us: "If you wish to be holy, behold thy mother; if you really wish that my kingdom will come, then behold thy mother; if you will to be rooted in goodness and be perfect as your heavenly Father is perfect, then behold thy mother."

Our Lord made no exception; His Mother was given to all—to those who sin, to those who mourn, and to those who suffer.

Are you a sinner? Then go to Mary, for she knows something of the bitterness of your soul. Mary knows what it is for a soul to be without Jesus, for during the three days' loss, she merited to become the Refuge of Sinners. She was meriting the honor anew at this very moment. She would never have been given to sinners had there not been a Crucifixion; there never would have been a Crucifixion without sin; and there never would have been sin without a sinner — and where sinners are, there are we. Mary, therefore, owes the dignity of her title to us, as sinners. Are you a sinner? Then hear her merciful Son lift you from despair with the words: "Behold thy mother."

Are you a mourner? Have you lost a sweet child, a kind father, a loving mother? Then you have lost only part of what you had. But Mary lost everything, for she lost God. To you, who mourn: "Behold thy mother."

In those moments of unbounded grief, when you are oppressed by your sins, and dripping tears from a wounded or broken heart; when you are sick of what you have and hunger after what you have not; when holiness seems such a distant goal and heaven so far off, then say to Mary: "Remember, Jesus said to thee, concerning me, as wicked as I am: 'Woman, behold thy son.'"

Thy Will Be Done on Earth as It Is in Heaven

My God, my God, why hast thou forsaken me?

—Matthew 27:46

In the Our Father, Our Lord asked us to resign ourselves to the will of the heavenly Father; on the Cross, He now resigned Himself to that same divine will. The real lesson hidden in these words is that now and then we face the unintelligible and mysterious things of life, and the only solution is to trust in the will of God. "Thy will be done on earth as it is in heaven." We ask ourselves such questions as: "Why should I suffer? Why did God take away my mother? Why is there pain? Why do the innocent suffer? Why does God abandon me?" There is no answer on earth except: "Thy will be done."

Our Lord in this word is reemphasizing the lesson taught in the book of Job. Job was sorely afflicted. He lost his children, his fortune; his wife turned against him, his friends abused him, and his whole body became afflicted with dread. And so he asked the question: "Why?"

"Why did I not die in the womb, why did I not perish when I came out of the belly, why was I received upon the knees, why was I suckled at the breasts; why is light given to him that is in misery and life to them that are in bitterness of soul?" (3:11–12, 20).

Job's friends tried to give him human explanations, to solve all of his riddles, to make everything reasonable, and to show how one part of the universe fits every other part. Now if the book of Job were a purely human document, a trivial poet or a modern dramatist would have made God enter the scene and answer the questions of Job. And yet when God does come on the scene, what does He actually do? He does not answer the questions of Job. He asks Job more questions in a way that abolishes all foolish questions. He turns to Job and says: "I will ask thee, and answer thou me. Where wast thou when I laid the foundations of the earth?… Upon what are its bases grounded? Or who laid the cornerstone thereof?… Who shut up the sea with doors, when it broke forth as issuing out of the womb: When I made a cloud the garment thereof and wrapped it in a mist as in swaddling bands?" (38:3–4, 6, 9).

"Then Job answered the Lord, and said: I know that thou canst do all things, and no thought is hid from thee.… Therefore I have spoken unwisely, and things that above measure exceeded my knowledge" (Job 42:1–3).

God insists on the inexplicableness of everything. The Maker of all things is astonished at the things He has made. Instead of proving to Job that it is a world explicable by science, He shows Job that it is a much stranger world than science ever suspected. The refusal of God to explain His design is itself a burning hint of His design: namely, the riddles of God are more satisfying than the solutions of men. And so, in the book of Job, we see he was tormented not because he was the worst of men but because he was the best. It was Good Friday that was prefigured in the wounds of Job.

The lesson for us is that many things are inexplicable here below, but they are only the details; for instance, "Why this pain?" "Why this loss?" "Why this sorrow?" The general principles remain true and unshakable: God is good, and He wills what is best for the soul. "My God, why hast thou forsaken me?" means forsaken only in appearance, not in reality. We may be lonely, but God is never out of our hearing. Our Lord has gone into the forests of suffering and loneliness, but He has left His footprints there, so we can find the way out. Take God's hand and follow Him in the dark, trusting and believing. We cannot say He does not know what it is to be abandoned, for He was abandoned on the Cross. "Trust Him when dark doubts assail thee; trust Him when trust is small; trust Him when simply to trust Him is the hardest thing of all."[1]

[1] From the hymn "Trust Him When Thy Doubts Are Many," stanza 5.

Give Us This Day Our Daily Bread

I thirst.

—John 19:28

"Daily bread." At Capernaum, Jesus ministered to the needs of men by giving them food for their bodies. He told men to pray for bread: "Give us this day our daily bread"; but at Calvary, He asks for a drink. Then He gave His gift to the multitude; now the multitude must give their gift. He had been the Giver; now He would be the Receiver. From a torn body, He cries, "I thirst." Thirst is the most impatient of all sufferings; there is an imperious urgency about it—a fierce sting.

But this was not just a cry for water. We know that once before, He asked the Samaritan woman for a drink, but when she drew the water from the well, there is no record that He took it. He was thirsting for her soul.

The lesson seems to be that God needs us. He is perfect, and yet He craves our love. He is all-powerful, and yet He is weak without our love. He is infinitely happy and yet unhappy without us. He is the Fountain of Everlasting Waters, and yet He cries, "I thirst." He does seem to need us. How? Not, of course, in the sense that He is imperfect or incomplete without us, but rather He needs us because we need Him.

The world is full of such examples. The charitable rich man thirsts for the poor. He does not need the poor man; from a worldly point of view, the poor man will take part of his substance. The poor man needs him only for food. But the rich man needs the poor man to exercise his charity. Truly can he say: "I thirst." I need you in order to be kind. In that sense, Our Lord thirsts for us because we need Him so.

He says to us: "I thirst" for you—you the unmortified because you need my spirit of sacrifice. You who would have a Calvary with hands unscarred and white have need of my hands, which are pierced and red. I am the Redeemer. To you who would never take up a cross, to you who need the spirit of penance, I cry: "I thirst." I thirst for you because your love of pleasure needs my love of sacrifice. I thirst for you because your love of the world needs my love of heaven. I do not thirst for you because I need you—for without you, I never would have had the Cross. I do not thirst for you because I need you for my happiness—for without you there would never have been sin. I thirst for you, not because I need you, but because you need me. Why, then, when I say, "I thirst," do you, like the soldier, offer me bitter vinegar and gall?

Forgive Us Our Trespasses as We Forgive Those Who Trespass against Us

It is consummated.

—John 19:30

Everyone who ever came into the world came into it to live. Our Lord, on the contrary, came not into it to live, but to die. His one supreme task was to lay down His life for the redemption of many. The forgiving of the trespasses of man by blotting out sin was the unique business His Father had assigned to Him. Now that duty was done. He had made it possible for us to pray: "Forgive us our trespasses as we forgive those who trespass against us," and so now He cries out with joy of victory won: "It is consummated."

God labored for six days in the creation of the world, and at the end of it came the divine applause of a work completed: "And God saw that it was good." For thirty-three years, God-made-man burned with desire to be baptized with the blood of redemption; and now, at the end of the three hours on the Cross, God saw once more "that it was good." It took only a word to create, but it took a life to redeem.

What a lesson for us! How few of us ever finish the tasks assigned to us! The world is full of souls that are like unfinished symphonies and half-completed Gothic cathedrals—souls who have begun the poem of their lives but have never written the last line; souls that paint pictures and leave out the borders; souls that never have the joy of looking on a perfect work, seeing that it is good, and then, catching an echo from the Cross, crying out the song of victory: "It is finished."

Calvary is a place of great impatience. Many souls follow Our Lord to the Mount of Beatitudes, but refuse to follow Him to Calvary; some carry their cross to Calvary, but when they get there, they lay it down; some are stripped of the garments of doubt but refuse to be nailed in the fullness of sacrifice; others are nailed but unfasten themselves before the elevation of the Cross; others are crucified but answer the challenge of the world and come down after one hour, after tfwo hours, within a minute of the sound of three. The world is full of half-crucified souls. Few there are who stay until the very end; few there are who know what it is to give all, to see the work well done and experience the thrill of a victory won. Would that there were a single day in our lives in which we could honestly say, "I have given God all! It is finished."

Seventh Word

Deliver Us from Evil

Father, into thy hands I commend my spirit.

—Luke 23:46

There is no deliverance from evil except in heaven. That, too, is why the final petition of the Our Father, which asks that we be delivered from evil, is balanced by the last words of Our Lord from the Cross, commending His Soul into the hands of His heavenly Father.

There is evil in the world, and as long as we remain here below, we must struggle against it. God might have made a different world, a world in which we would have sprouted virtue by the same necessity that the sun rises, and fire burns, and iron is hard. But then where would merit and character have been? All life is a trial. I can be one of God's heroes only because I might have been one of God's cowards; I can be one of the patriots of the kingdom of God only because I might have been one of its traitors; I can be a saint of the Cross only because I might also be a devil. There is no epic of the certainties of life; no crowns of merit rest suspended over those who do not fight; there are no aureoles except for those who might have turned back and yet pushed on.

Christ's eyes now look downward as the last few drops of blood reluctantly wed themselves to the rocks, splitting them open like hungry mouths. There is always a strange power in the eyes of the dying that enables them to follow the ones they love, even when other senses are mute and dead. His eyes are now resting on the same object they rested on when He was born — His sweet and beloved Mother. She felt His eyes fixed on her. She looked up, the eyes closed, the head dropped, there was the rupture of a heart through the rapture of love, and there Mary stood beneath the Cross — a childless Mother, bereaved of God.

Sleep on, tired world! Your God is dead. Sleep on, creatures! You now have creation to yourself. Sleep on, Jerusalem! You have slain the Prophet who would have made you a Heavenly City. Sleep on, sinners! The heart that filled you with remorse is pierced with a lance. Sleep on, all you who hate, for the wings of love are broken. Sleep on, atheists; you have killed your God. Sleep in your false sleep — you can do more than nature can, for it wakes and shudders at your crime. Sleep on for your few brief moments, but remember, someday you will awaken, and one vision will meet your eyes: the vision of Love crucified on a Cross.

May you throw yourself beneath it, and in the ecstasy of knowing God as your Father, may you pray the prayer of salvation: "Our Father, who art in heaven — like Thy Son — into Thy hands I commend my spirit."

2

Calvary and the Mass:
A Missal Companion

Prologue

There are certain things in life that are too beautiful to be forgotten, such as the love of a mother. Hence, we treasure her picture. The love of soldiers who sacrificed themselves for their country is likewise too beautiful to be forgotten; hence, we revere their memory on Memorial Day. But the greatest blessing that ever came to this earth was the visitation of the Son of God in the form and habit of man. His life, above all lives, is too beautiful to be forgotten; hence, we treasure the divinity of His Words in Sacred Scripture and the charity of His deeds in our daily actions. Unfortunately, this is all some souls remember—His Words and His *deeds*; important as these are, they are not the greatest characteristic of the Divine Savior.

The most sublime act in the history of Christ was His *death*. Death is always important, for it seals a destiny. Any dying man is a scene. Any dying scene is a sacred place. That is why the great literature of the past, which has touched on the emotions surrounding death, has never passed out of date. But of all deaths in the record of man, none was more important than the death of Christ. Everyone else who was born into the world, came into it to *live*; Our Lord came into it to *die*. Death was a stumbling block to the life of Socrates, but it was the crown to the life of Christ. He Himself told us that He came "to give his life [as a] redemption for many"; that no one could take away His Life; but He would lay it down of Himself (Matt. 20:28; John 10:18).

If, then, death was the supreme moment for which Christ lived, it was therefore the *one thing* He wished to have remembered. He did not ask that men should write down His Words; He did not ask that His kindness to the poor should be recorded in history; but He did ask that men remember His death. And in order that its memory might not be any haphazard narrative on the part of men, He Himself instituted the precise way it should be recalled.

The memorial was instituted the night before He died, at what has since been called the Last Supper. Taking bread into His hands, He said: "This is my body, which shall be delivered for you"—that is, delivered unto death. Then, over the chalice of wine, He said, "This is my blood of the new testament, which shall be shed for many unto remission of sins." (see Luke 22:19; Matt. 26:28). Thus, in an unbloody symbol of the parting of the blood from the body, by the separate consecration of bread and wine, did Christ pledge Himself to death in the sight of God and men and represent His death, which was to come the next afternoon at three.[2] He was offering Himself as a Victim to be immolated, and that men might never forget that "greater love than this no man hath, that a man lay down his life for his friends" (John 15:13), He gave the divine

---

[2] "Death is put before us in a symbol, by means of that sacramental parting of the Blood from the Body; but death at the same time already pledged to God for all its worth, as well as all its awful reality, by the expressive language of the Sacred Symbol. The price of our sins shall be paid down on Calvary, but here the liability is incurred by our Redeemer and sub-scribed in His very Blood." Maurice de la Taille, S.J., *Catholic Faith in the Holy Eucharist*, p. 115. "There were not two distinct and complete sacrifices offered by Christ, one in the Cenacle, the other on Calvary. There was a sacrifice at the Last Supper, but it was the sacrifice of Redemption, and there was a sacrifice on the Cross, but it was the selfsame sacrifice continued and completed. The Supper and the Cross made up one complete sacrifice." Maurice de la Taille, S.J., *The Mystery of Faith and Human Opinion* (London: Sheed and Ward, 1930), p. 232.

command to the Church: "Do this for a commemoration of me" (Luke 22:19).

The following day, that which He had prefigured and foreshadowed, He realized in its completeness, as He was crucified between two thieves and His blood drained from His body for the redemption of the world.

The Church, which Christ founded, has not only preserved the Word He spoke, and the wonders He wrought; it has also taken Him seriously when He said: "Do this for a commemoration of me." And that action whereby we reenact His death on the Cross is the Sacrifice of the Mass, in which we do as a memorial what He did at the Last Supper as the prefiguration of His Passion.[3]

Hence, the Mass is to us the crowning act of Christian worship. A pulpit in which the words of Our Lord are repeated does not unite us to Him; a choir in which sweet sentiments are sung brings us no closer to His Cross than to His garments. A temple without an altar of sacrifice is nonexistent among primitive peoples and is meaningless among Christians. And so, in the Catholic Church, the *altar*, and not the pulpit or the choir or the organ, is the center of worship, for there is reenacted the memorial of His Passion. Its value does not depend on him who says it, or on him who hears it; it depends on Him who is the One High Priest and Victim, Jesus Christ Our Lord. With Him we are united, in spite

---

[3] "He offered the Victim to be immolated; we offer it as immolated of old. We offer the eternal Victim of the Cross, once made and forever enduring.... The Mass is a sacrifice because it is our oblation of the Victim once immolated, even as the Supper was the oblation of the Victim to be immolated." Taille, *The Mystery of Faith and Human Opinion*, pp. 239–240. The Mass is not only a commemoration; it is a living representation of the Sacrifice of the Cross. "In this Divine Sacrifice, which takes place at the Mass is contained and immolated, in an unbloody manner, the same Christ that was offered once for all in the blood upon the Cross.... It is one and the same Victim, one and the same High Priest, who made the offering through the ministry of His priests today, after having offered Himself upon the cross yesterday; only the manner of the oblation is different" (Council of Trent, Session 22).

of our nothingness; in a certain sense, we lose our individuality for the time being; we unite our intellect and our will, our heart and our soul, our body and our blood, so intimately with Christ that the heavenly Father sees not so much us with our imperfection, but sees us *in Him*, the Beloved Son in whom He is well pleased. The Mass is, for that reason, the greatest event in the history of mankind—the only Holy Act that keeps the wrath of God from a sinful world, because it holds the Cross between heaven and earth, thus renewing that decisive moment when our sad and tragic humanity journeyed suddenly forth to the fullness of supernatural life.

What is important at this point is that we take the proper mental attitude toward the Mass and remember this important fact: that the Sacrifice of the Cross is not something that happened hundreds of years ago. It is still happening. It is not something past, like the signing of the Declaration of Independence; it is an abiding drama on which the curtain has not yet rung down. Let it not be believed that it happened a long time ago and therefore concerns us no more than anything else in the past. *Calvary belongs to all times and to all places.* That is why, when our Blessed Lord ascended the heights of Calvary, He was fittingly stripped of His garments: He would save the world without the trappings of a passing world. His garments belonged to time, for they localized Him and fixed Him as a dweller in Galilee. Now that He was shorn of them and utterly dispossessed of earthly things, He belonged not to Galilee, not to a Roman province, but to the world. He became the universal poor man of the world, belonging to no one people, but to all men.

To express further the universality of the Redemption, the Cross was erected at the crossroads of civilization, at a central point between the three great cultures of Jerusalem, Rome, and Athens, in whose names He was crucified. The Cross was thus placarded before the eyes of men, to arrest the careless, to appeal to the thoughtless, to arouse the worldly. It was the one inescapable fact that the cultures and civilizations of His day could not resist. It is also the one inescapable fact of our day, which we cannot resist.

Prologue

The figures at the Cross were symbols of all who crucify. We were there in our representatives. What we are doing now to the Mystical Christ, they were doing in our names to the historical Christ. If we are envious of the good, we were there in the scribes and the Pharisees. If we are fearful of losing some temporal advantage by embracing Divine Truth and Love, we were there in Pilate. If we trust in material forces and seek to conquer through the world instead of through the spirit, we were there in Herod. And so the story goes on for the typical sins of the world. They all blind us to the fact that He is God. There was, therefore, a kind of inevitability about the Crucifixion. Men who were free to sin were also free to crucify.

As long as there is sin in the world, the Crucifixion is a reality. As the poet Rachel Annand Taylor has put it:

> I saw the son of man go by,
> Crowned with a crown of thorns.
> "Was it not finished Lord," said I,
> "And all the anguish borne?"
>
> He turned on me His awful eyes;
> "Hast Thou not understood?
> So every soul is a Calvary
> And every sin a rood."[4]

We were there, then, during that Crucifixion. The drama was already completed as far as the vision of Christ was concerned, but it had not yet been unfolded to all men and all places and all times. If a motion-picture reel, for example, were conscious of itself, it would know the drama from beginning to end, but the spectators in the theater would not know it until they had seen it unrolled upon the screen. In like manner, Our Lord on the Cross saw in His eternal mind the whole drama of history, the story of each individual soul and how, later on, it would react to His

---

4   Rachel A. Taylor, "The Question."

Crucifixion; but though He saw all, we could not know how we would react to the Cross until we were unrolled upon the screen of time. We were not conscious of being present there on Calvary that day, but He was conscious of our presence. Today we know the role we played in the theater of Calvary, by the way we live and act now in the theater of our day.

That is why Calvary is actual; why the Cross is the crisis; why, in a certain sense, the scars are still open; why pain still stands deified, and why blood like falling stars is still dropping upon our souls. There is no escaping the Cross, not even by denying it, as the Pharisees did; not even by selling Christ, as Judas did; not even by crucifying Him, as the executioners did. We all see it, either to embrace it in salvation or to fly from it into misery.

But how is it made visible? Where shall we find Calvary perpetuated? We shall find Calvary renewed, reenacted, re-presented, as we have seen, in the Mass. Calvary is one with the Mass, and the Mass is one with Calvary, for in both there is the same Priest and Victim. The Seven Last Words are like the seven parts of the Mass. And just as there are seven notes in music admitting an infinite variety of harmonies and combinations, so, too, on the Cross there are seven divine notes, which the dying Christ rang down the centuries, all of which combine to form the beautiful harmony of the world's redemption.

Each word is a part of the Mass. The first word, "Forgive," is the Confiteor; the second word, "This day you shall be with me in paradise," is the Offertory; the third word, "Behold thy Mother," is the Sanctus; the fourth word, "Why hast Thou abandoned me?," is the Consecration; the fifth word, "I thirst," is the Communion; the sixth word, "It is finished," is the Ite, Missa Est; the seventh word, "Father, into Thy hands I commend my spirit," is the Last Gospel.[5]

Picture, then, the High Priest Christ leaving the sacristy of heaven for the altar of Calvary. He has already put on the vestment of our human

---

[5] The prologue of the Gospel of St. John, read at the end of the Extraordinary Form of the Mass.

nature, the maniple of our suffering, the stole of priesthood, the chasuble of the Cross. Calvary is His cathedral; the rock of Calvary is the altar stone; the sun turning to red is the sanctuary lamp; Mary and John are the living side altars; the Host is His Body; the wine is His Blood. He is upright as Priest, yet He is prostrate as Victim. His Mass is about to begin.

The Confiteor

Father, forgive them, for they know not what they do.

—Luke 23:34

The Mass begins with the Confiteor. The Confiteor is a prayer in which we confess our sins and ask the Blessed Mother and the saints to intercede to God for our forgiveness, for only the clean of heart can see God. Our Blessed Lord also begins His Mass with the Confiteor. But His Confiteor differs from ours in this: He has no sins to confess. He is God and therefore is sinless. "Which of you shall convince me of sin?" (John 8:46). His Confiteor, then, cannot be a prayer for the forgiveness of *His* sins, but it can be a prayer for the forgiveness of our sins.

Others would have screamed, cursed, and wrestled as the nails pierced their hands and feet. But no vindictiveness finds place in the Savior's breast; no appeal comes from His lips for vengeance on His murderers; He breathes no prayer for strength to bear His pain. Incarnate Love forgets injury, forgets pain, and in that moment of concentrated agony, reveals something of the height, the depth, and the breadth of the wonderful love of God as He says His Confiteor: "Father, forgive them, for they know not what they do."

He did not say, "Forgive me," but "Forgive them." The moment of death was certainly the one most likely to produce confession of sin, for conscience in the last solemn hours does assert its authority; and yet not a single sigh of penitence escaped His lips. He was associated with sinners but never associated with sin. In death as well as life, He was unconscious of a single unfulfilled duty to His heavenly Father. And why? Because a sinless Man is not just a man; He is more than mere man. He is sinless because He is God—and there is the difference. We draw our prayers from the depths of our consciousness of sin: He drew His silence from His own intrinsic sinlessness. That one word *forgive* proves Him to be the Son of God.

Notice the grounds on which He asked His heavenly Father to forgive us—"because they know not what they do." When anyone injures us or blames us wrongly, we say: "They should have known better." But when we sin against God, He finds an excuse for forgiveness—our ignorance.

There is no redemption for the fallen angels. The blood drops that fell from the Cross on Good Friday in that Mass of Christ did not touch the spirits of the fallen angels. Why? Because they knew what they were doing. They saw all the consequences of their acts, just as clearly as we see that two and two make four, or that a thing cannot exist and not exist at the same time. Truths of this kind when understood, cannot be taken back; they are irrevocable and eternal. Hence, when they decided to rebel against Almighty God, there was no taking back the decision. They knew what they were doing!

But with us, it is different. We do not see the consequences of our acts as clearly as the angels do; we are weaker; we are ignorant. But if we did know that every sin of pride wove a crown of thorns for the head of Christ; if we knew that every contradiction of His divine command made for Him the sign of contradiction, the Cross; if we knew that every grasping avaricious act nailed His hands, and every journey into the byways of sin dug His feet; if we knew how good God is and still went on sinning, we would never be saved. It is only our ignorance of the infinite love of the Sacred Heart that brings us within the hearing of His Confiteor from the Cross: "Father, forgive them, for they know not what they do."

These words, let it be deeply graven on our souls, do not constitute an excuse for continued sin, but a motive for contrition and penance. Forgiveness is not a denial of sin. Our Lord does not deny the horrible fact of sin, and that is where the modern world is wrong. It explains sin away: it ascribes it to a fall in the evolutionary process, to a survival of ancient taboos; it identifies it with psychological verbiage.

In a word, the modern world denies sin. Our Lord reminds us that it is the most terrible of all realities. Otherwise, why does it give Sinlessness a cross? Why does it shed innocent blood? Why does it have such awful associations: blindness, compromise, cowardice, hatred, and cruelty? Why does it now lift itself out of the realm of the impersonal and assert itself as personal by nailing Innocence to a gibbet? An abstraction cannot do that. But sinful man can.

Hence, He who loved men unto death allowed sin to wreak its vengeance upon Him, in order that they might forever understand its horror as the crucifixion of Him who loved them most.

There is no denial of sin here—and yet, with all its horror, the Victim forgives. In that one and the same event, there is the sign of sin's utter depravity and the seal of divine forgiveness. From that point on, no man can look upon a crucifix and say that sin is not serious, nor can he ever say that it cannot be forgiven. By the way He suffered, He revealed the reality of sin; by the way, He bore it, He shows His mercy toward the sinner.

It is the Victim who has suffered that forgives: and in that combination of a Victim so humanly beautiful, so divinely loving, so wholly innocent, does one find a great crime and a greater forgiveness. Under the shelter of the blood of Christ, the worst sinners may take their stand; for there is a power in that blood to turn back the tides of vengeance that threaten to drown the world.

The world will give you sin explained away, but only on Calvary do you experience the divine contradiction of sin forgiven. On the Cross, supreme self-giving and divine love transform sin's worst act in the noblest deed and sweetest prayer the world has ever seen or heard, the Confiteor of Christ: "Father, forgive them, for they know not what they do."

That word *forgive*, which rang out from the Cross that day when sin rose to its full strength and then fell defeated by Love, did not die with its echo. Not long before, that same merciful Savior had taken means to prolong forgiveness through space and time, even to the consummation of the world. Gathering the nucleus of His Church round about Him, He said to His Apostles: "Whose sins you shall forgive, they are forgiven" (John 20:23).

Somewhere in the world today, then, the successors of the Apostles have the power to forgive. It is not for us to ask: But how can man forgive sins? For man cannot forgive sins. But God can forgive sins *through* man, for is not that the way God forgave His executioners from the Cross—through the instrumentality of His human nature?

Why, then, is it not reasonable to expect Him still to forgive sins through other human natures to whom He gave that power? And where find those human natures?

You know the story of the box, which was long ignored and even ridiculed as worthless; and one day it was opened and found to contain the great heart of a giant. In every Catholic church, that box exists. We call it the confessional box. It is ignored and ridiculed by many, but in it is to be found the Sacred Heart of the forgiving Christ, forgiving sinners through the uplifted hand of His priest, as He once forgave through His own uplifted hands on the Cross. There is only one forgiveness—the forgiveness of God. There is only one "Forgive"—the "Forgive" of an eternal divine act in which we come in contact at various moments of time.

As the air is always filled with symphony and speech, but we do not hear it unless we tune it in on our radios, so neither do souls feel the joy of that eternal and divine "Forgive" unless they are attuned to it in time; and the confessional box is the place where we tune in to that cry from the Cross.

Would to God that our modern mind, instead of denying the guilt, would look to the Cross, admit its guilt, and seek forgiveness; would that those who have uneasy consciences that worry them in the light and haunt them in the darkness, would seek relief, not on the plane of medicine but on the plane of divine justice; would that they who tell the dark secrets of their minds would do so not for the sake of sublimation but for the sake of purgation; would that those poor mortals who shed tears in silence would find an absolving hand to wipe them away.

Must it be forever true that the greatest tragedy of life is not what happens to souls, but rather what souls miss? And what greater tragedy is there than to miss the peace of sin forgiven? The Confiteor is, at the foot of the altar, our cry of unworthiness: the Confiteor from the Cross is our hope of pardon and absolution. The wounds of the Savior were terrible, but the worst wound of all would be to be unmindful that we caused it all. The Confiteor can save us from that, for it is an admission that there is something to be forgiven—and more than we shall ever know.

There is a story told of a nun who was one day dusting a small image of Our Blessed Lord in the chapel. In the course of her duty, she let it slip to the floor. She picked it up undamaged, kissed it, and put it back again in its place, saying, "If you had never fallen, you never would have received that." I wonder if our Blessed Lord does not feel the same way about us, for if we had never sinned, we never could call Him "Savior."

The Offertory

Amen I say to thee, this day thou shalt be with me in paradise.

—Luke 23:43

This is now the Offertory of the Mass, for Our Lord is offering Himself to His heavenly Father. But in order to remind us that He is offered not alone, but in union with us, He unites with His offertory the soul of the thief at the right. To make His ignominy more complete, in a masterstroke of malice, they crucified Him between two thieves. He walked among sinners during His life, so now they let Him hang between them at death. But He changed the picture and made the two thieves the symbols of the sheep and the goats, which will stand at His right and left hand when He comes in the clouds of heaven, with His then triumphant Cross, to judge both the living and the dead.

Both thieves at first reviled and blasphemed, but one of them, whom tradition calls Dismas, turned his head to read the meekness and dignity on the face of the crucified Savior. As a piece of coal thrown into the fire is transformed into a bright and glowing thing, so the black soul of this thief thrown into the fires of the Crucifixion glowed with love for the Sacred Heart.

While the thief on the left was saying: "If thou be Christ, save thyself and us," the repentant thief rebuked him saying: "Neither dost thou fear

God, seeing thou art under the same condemnation. And we indeed justly, for we receive the due reward of our deeds; but this man hath done no evil." That same thief then emitted a plea, not for a place in the seats of the mighty, but only not to be forgotten: "Remember me, when thou shalt come into thy kingdom" (Luke 23:39–43).

Such sorrow and faith must not go unrewarded. At a moment when the power of Rome could not make Him speak, when His friends thought all was lost, and His enemies believed all was won, Our Lord broke the silence. He who was the accused became the Judge: He who was the crucified became the Divine Assessor of souls. As to the penitent thief, He trumpeted the words: "This day thou shalt be with me in paradise." This day — when you said your first prayer and your last; this day — thou shalt be with me — and where I am, there is paradise.

With these words, Our Lord, who was offering Himself to His heavenly Father as the great Host, now unites with Him on the paten of the Cross the first small host ever offered in the Mass, the host of the repentant thief, a brand plucked from the burning, a sheaf torn from the earthly reapers; the wheat ground in the mill of the Crucifixion and made bread for the Eucharist.

Our Lord does not suffer alone on the Cross: He suffers with us. That is why He united the sacrifice of the thief with His own. It is this that St. Paul means when he says that we should fill up those things that are wanting to the sufferings of Christ. This does not mean Our Lord on the Cross did not suffer all He could. It means, rather, that the physical, historical Christ suffered all He could in His own human nature, but that the Mystical Christ, which is Christ and us, has not suffered to *our* fullness. All the other good thieves in the history of the world have not yet admitted their wrong and pleaded for remembrances. Our Lord is now in heaven. He, therefore, can suffer no more in His human nature, but He can suffer more in our human natures.

So He reaches out to other human natures, to yours and mine, and asks us to do as the thief did — namely, to incorporate ourselves to Him on the Cross, so that, sharing in His Crucifixion, we might also share in His Resurrection, and so that, made partakers of His Cross, we might also be made partakers of His glory in heaven.

As our Blessed Lord on that day chose the thief as the small host of sacrifice, He chooses us today as the other small hosts united with Him on the paten of the altar. Go back in your mind's eye to a Mass, to any Mass that was celebrated in the first centuries of the Church, before civilization became completely financial and economic. If we went to the Holy Sacrifice in the early Church, we would have brought to the altar each morning some bread and some wine. The priest would have used one piece of that unleavened bread and some of that wine for the sacrifice of the Mass. The rest would have been put aside, blessed, and distributed to the poor. Today we do not bring bread and wine. We bring its equivalent: we bring that which buys bread and wine. Hence the Offertory collection.

Why do we bring bread and wine or its equivalent to the Mass? We bring bread and wine because these two things, of all things in nature, most represent the substance of life. Wheat is as the very marrow of the ground, and the grapes its very blood, both of which give us the body and blood of life. In bringing those two things, which give us life, nourish us, *we are equivalently bringing ourselves to* the Sacrifice of the Mass.

We are therefore present at each and every Mass under the appearance of bread and wine, which stand as symbols of our body and blood. We are not passive spectators as we might be watching a spectacle in a theater, but we are co-offering our Mass with Christ. If any picture adequately describes our role in this drama, it is this: There is a great cross before us on which is stretched the great Host, Christ. Round about the hill of Calvary are our small crosses on which we, the small hosts, are to be offered. When Our Lord goes to His Cross, we go to our little crosses, and offer ourselves in union with Him, as a clean oblation to the heavenly Father.

At that moment, we literally fulfill to the smallest detail the Savior's command: Take up your cross daily and follow me. In doing so, He is not asking us to do anything He has not already done Himself. Nor is it any excuse to say: "I am a poor, unworthy host." So was the thief.

Note that there were two attitudes in the soul of that thief, both of which made him acceptable to Our Lord. The first was the recognition of the fact that He deserved what He was suffering but that the sinless Christ did not deserve His Cross; in other words, he was *penitent*. The second was *faith* in Him whom men rejected, but whom the thief recognized as the very King of Kings.

Upon what conditions do we become small hosts in the Mass? How does our sacrifice become one with Christ's and as acceptable as the thief's? Only by reproducing in our souls the two attitudes in the soul of the thief: *penitence* and *faith*.

First of all, we must be penitent with the thief and say: "I deserve punishment for my sins. I stand in need of sacrifice." Some of us do not know how wicked or how ungrateful to God we are. If we did, we would not so complain about the shocks and pains of life. Our consciences are like darkened rooms from which light has been long excluded. We draw the curtain and lo! everywhere what we thought was cleanliness, we now find dust.

Some consciences have been so filmed over with excuses that they pray with the Pharisee: "I thank Thee, O God, that I am not as the rest of men" (see Luke 18:11). Others blaspheme the God of heaven for their pain and sins but do not repent. The World War, for example, was meant to be a purgation of evil; it was meant to teach us that we cannot get along without God, but the world refused to learn the lesson. Like the thief on the left, it refuses to be penitent: it refuses to see any relation of justice between sin and sacrifice, between rebellion and a cross.

But the more penitent we are, the less anxious we are to escape our crosses. The more we see ourselves as we are, the more we say with the good thief: "I deserved this cross." He did not want to be excused; he did not want to have his sin explained away; he did not want to be let off; he did not ask to be taken down. He wanted only to be forgiven. He was willing even to be a small host on his own little cross—but that was because he was penitent. Nor is there given to us any other way to become little hosts with Christ in the Mass than by breaking our hearts with sorrow; for unless we admit we are wounded, how can we feel the need of healing? Unless we are sorry for our part in the Crucifixion, how can we ever ask to be forgiven its sin?

The second condition of becoming a host in the Offertory of the Mass is faith. The thief looked above the head of our Blessed Lord and saw a sign that read "King." Strange king that! For a crown: thorns. For royal purple: His own blood. For a throne: a cross. For courtiers: executioners. For a coronation: a crucifixion. And yet beneath all that dross, the thief saw the gold; amid all those blasphemies, he prayed.

His faith was so strong that he was content to remain on his cross. The thief on the left asked to be taken down, but not the thief on the right. Why? Because he knew there were greater evils than crucifixions and another life beyond the cross. He had faith in the Man on the central Cross, who could have turned thorns into garlands and nails into rosebuds if He willed; but he had faith in a kingdom beyond the Cross, knowing that the sufferings of this world are not worthy to be compared with the joys that are to come. With the psalmist, his soul cried: "Though I should walk in the midst of the shadow of death, I will fear no evils, for thou art with me" (Ps. 22 [23]:4).

Such faith was like that of the three youths in the fiery furnace who were commanded by the king, Nebuchadnezzar, to adore the golden statue. Their answer was: "For behold, our God, whom we worship, is able to save us from the furnace of burning fire, and to deliver us out of thy hands, O king. But if He will not, be it known to thee, O king, that we will not worship thy gods, nor adore the golden statue which thou hast set up" (Dan. 3:17–18). Note that they did not ask God to deliver them from the fiery furnace, though they knew God could do it, "for He is able to save us from the furnace of burning fire." They left themselves wholly in God's hands, and like Job, they trusted Him.

So, likewise, with the good thief: He knew Our Lord could deliver Him. But *he did not ask to be taken down from the cross*, for Our Lord did not come down Himself, even though the mob challenged Him. The thief would be a small host, if need be, unto the very end of the Mass.

This did not mean the thief did not love life: He loved life as much as we love it. He wanted life and a long life, and he found it, for what life is longer than life eternal? To each and every one of us, in like manner, it is given to discover that eternal life. But there is no other way to enter it than by penance and by faith, which unite us to that Great Host—the Priest and Victim Christ. Thus do we become spiritual thieves and steal heaven once again.

The Sanctus

Woman, behold thy son. . . . Behold thy mother.

—John 19:26–27

Five days ago, our Blessed Lord made a triumphal entry into the city of Jerusalem: triumphant cries rang about His ears; palms dropped beneath His feet, as the air resounded with hosannas to the Son of David and praises to the Holy One of Israel. As for those who would have silenced the demonstration in His honor, Our Lord reminds them that if their voices were silent, even the very stones would have cried out. That was the birthday of Gothic cathedrals.

They did not know the real reason they were calling Him *holy*; they did not even understand why He accepted the tribute of their praise. They thought that they were proclaiming Him a kind of earthly king. But He accepted their demonstration because He was going to be the King of a spiritual empire. He accepted their tributes, their hosannas, and their paeans of praise because He was going to His cross as a Victim. And every victim must be holy: *sanctus, sanctus, sanctus*. Five days later came the Sanctus of the Mass of Calvary. But at that Sanctus of His Mass, He does not say "holy"—He speaks to the holy ones; He does not whisper "Sanctus"—He addresses Himself *to* saints, to His sweet Mother Mary, and His beloved disciple, John.

Striking words they are: "Woman, behold thy son.... Behold thy mother." He was speaking now to saints. He had no need of saintly intercession, for He was the Holy One of God. But we have need of holiness, for every victim of the Mass must be holy, undefiled, and unpolluted. But how can we be holy participants in the Sacrifice of the Mass? Christ gives the answer: by putting ourselves under the protection of His Blessed Mother. He addresses the Church and all her members in the person of John and says to each of us: "Behold thy mother." That is why He addressed her not as "Mother" but as "Woman." She had a universal mission, to be not only His Mother but the Mother of all Christians. She had been His Mother; now she was to be the Mother of His Mystical Body, the Church. And we were to be her children.

There is a tremendous mystery hidden in that one word *Woman*. It was really the last lesson in detachment that Jesus had been teaching her these many years and the first lesson of the new attachment. Our Lord had been gradually "alienating," as it were, His affections from His Mother, not in the sense that she was to love Him less, or that He was to love her less, but only in the sense that she was to love us more. She was to be detached from motherhood in the flesh, only to be more attached to that greater motherhood in the spirit. Hence the word *Woman*. She was to make us *other Christs*, for as Mary had raised the Holy One of God, so only she could raise us as holy ones for God, worthy to say, "Sanctus, sanctus, sanctus," in the Mass of that prolonged Calvary.

The story of the preparation for her role as Mother of the Mystical Body of Christ is unfolded in three scenes in the life of her Divine Son, each one suggesting the lesson that Calvary itself was to reveal: namely, that she was called to be not only the Mother of God but also the Mother of men; not only the Mother of holiness but the Mother of those who ask to be holy.

The first scene took place in the Temple, where Mary and Joseph found Jesus after a three-day search. The Blessed Mother reminds Him that their hearts were broken with sorrow during the long search, and He answers: "Did you not know that I must be about my Father's business?" (Luke 2:49). Here He was equivalently saying: "I have another business,

Mother, than the business of the carpenter shop. My Father has sent me into this world on the supreme business of Redemption, to make all men adopted sons of my heavenly Father in the greater kingdom of the brotherhood of Christ." How far the full vision of those words dawned upon Mary we know not; whether she then understood that the Fatherhood of God meant that she was to be the Mother of men, we know not. But certainly, eighteen years later, in the second scene, the marriage feast of Cana, she came to a fuller understanding of that mission.

What a consoling thought it is to think that our Blessed Lord, who talked penance, who preached mortification, who insisted upon taking up the cross daily and following Him, should have begun His public life by assisting at a wedding festival! What a beautiful understanding of our hearts!

When, in the course of the banquet, the wine was exhausted, Mary, always interested in others, was the first to notice and the first to seek relief from the embarrassment. She simply said to our Blessed Lord, "They have no wine." And our Blessed Lord said to her, "Woman, what is that to me and to thee? My hour is not yet come" (John 2:3-4). "Woman, what is that to me?" He did not call her "Mother," but "Woman"—the same title she was to receive three years later.

He was equivalently saying to her: "You are asking me to do something which belongs to me as the Son of God. You are asking me to work a miracle, which only God can work; you are asking me to exercise my divinity, which has relationship to all mankind—namely, as its Redeemer. But once that divinity operates for the salvation of the world, you become not only my Mother but the Mother of redeemed humanity. Your physical motherhood passes into the wider world of spiritual motherhood, and for that reason, I call you 'Woman.'" And in order to prove that her intercession is powerful in that role of universal motherhood, He ordered the pots filled with water, and in the language of Richard Crashaw, the first miracle was worked: "the conscious waters saw their God and blushed."[6]

[6] *Epigrammatum sacrorum liber* (1634).

The third scene happens within two years. One day, as Our Lord was preaching, someone interrupted His discourse to say, "Thy mother ... stands without, seeking thee." Our Blessed Lord said, "Who is my mother?" and stretching forth His hands toward His disciples He said: "Behold my mother and my brethren. For whosoever shall do the will of my Father, that is in heaven, he is my brother, and my sister, and mother" (see Matt. 12:47, 49–50). The meaning was unmistakable. There is such a thing as spiritual maternity; there are bonds other than those of the flesh; there are ties other than the ties of blood—namely, spiritual ties that band together those of the kingdom where reign the Fatherhood of God and the Brotherhood of Christ.

These three scenes have their climax at the Cross, where Mary is called "Woman." It was the second Annunciation. The angel said to her in the first: "Hail, Mary." Her Son speaks to her in the second: "Woman." This did not mean she ceased to be His Mother; she is always the Mother of God, but her motherhood enlarged and expanded; it became spiritual, it became universal, for at that moment she became our mother. Our Lord created the bond where it did not exist by nature, as only He could do.

And how did she become the mother of men? By becoming not only the mother but also the spouse of Christ. He was the new Adam; she is the new Eve. And as Adam and Eve brought forth their natural progeny, which we are, so Christ and His Mother brought forth at the Cross their spiritual progeny, which we are: children of Mary and members of the Mystical Body of Christ. She brought forth her Firstborn in Bethlehem. Note that St. Luke calls Our Lord the *Firstborn*—not because our Blessed Mother was to have other children *according to the flesh*, but only because she was to have other children *according to the spirit*. That moment when our Blessed Lord said to her, "Woman," she became in a certain sense the spouse of Christ, and she brought forth in sorrow her firstborn in the spirit, and his name was John. Who the second-born was we know not. It might have been Peter. It might have been Andrew. But we, at any rate, are the millionth-and-millionth-born of that woman at the foot of the Cross. It was a poor exchange indeed, receiving the son of Zebedee in place of the Son of God. But surely our gain was greater, for while she acquired but undutiful and often rebellious children, we obtained the most loving Mother in the world — the Mother of Jesus.

We are children of Mary — literally, *children*. She is our Mother, not by title of fiction, not by title of courtesy; she is our Mother because she endured at that particular moment the pains of childbirth for all of us. And why did Our Lord give her to us as mother? Because He knew *we could never be holy without her*. He came to us through her purity, and only through her purity can we go back to her. There is no Sanctus apart from Mary. Every victim that mounts that altar under the species of bread and wine must have said the Confiteor and become a holy victim — but there is no holiness without Mary.

Note that when that word was spoken to our Blessed Mother, there was another woman there who was prostrate. Have you ever noticed that practically every traditional representation of the Crucifixion always pictures Magdalene on her knees at the foot of the Cross? But you have never yet seen an image of the Blessed Mother prostrate. John was there, and he tells in his Gospel that she stood. He saw her stand. But why did she stand? She stood to be of service to us. She stood to be our minister, our Mother.

If Mary could have prostrated herself at that moment as Magdalene did, if she could have only wept, her sorrow would have had an outlet. The sorrow that cries is never the sorrow that breaks the heart. It is the heart that can find no outlet in the fountain of tears that cracks; it is the heart that cannot have an emotional breakdown that breaks. And all that sorrow was part of our purchase price paid by our Co-Redemptrix, Mary, the Mother of God!

Because Our Lord willed her to us as our Mother, He left her on this earth after He ascended into heaven, in order that she might mother the infant Church. The infant Church had need of a mother, just as the infant Christ did. She had to remain on earth until her family had grown. That is why we find her on Pentecost abiding in prayer with the Apostles, awaiting the descent of the Holy Spirit. She was mothering the Mystical Body of Christ.

Now she is crowned in heaven as Queen of Angels and Saints, turning heaven into another marriage feast of Cana when she intercedes with her Divine Savior on behalf of us, her other children, brothers of Christ and sons of the heavenly Father.

Virgin Mother! What a beautiful conjunction of virginity and motherhood, one supplying the defect of the other. Virginity alone lacks something: there is an incompleteness about it; something unfulfilled; a faculty unused. Motherhood alone loses something: there is a surrender, an unflowering, a plucking of a blossom. Oh! For a *rapprochement* in which there would be a virginity that never lacked anything and a motherhood that never lost anything! We have both in Mary, the Virgin Mother: Virgin by the overshadowing of the Holy Spirit in Bethlehem and Pentecost; Mother by the millions of her progeny, from Jesus unto you and me.

There is no question here of confusing Our Lady and Our Lord. We venerate our Mother; we worship Our Lord. We ask of Jesus those things that only God can give: mercy, grace, and forgiveness. We ask that Mary should intercede for us with Him, and especially at the hour of our death. Because of her nearness to Jesus, which her vocation involves, we know Our Lord listens especially to her appeal. To no other saint can we speak as a child to his mother: no other virgin, or martyr, or mother, or confessor has ever suffered as much for us as she has; no one has ever established better claim to our love and patronage than she has.

As Jesus came to us through her, all favors come to us from Jesus through her, as the Mediatrix of all graces. We wish to be holy, but we know there is no holiness without her, for she was the gift of Jesus to us at the Sanctus of His Cross. No woman can ever forget the child of her womb; so certainly Mary can never forget us. That is why we feel, way, down deep in our hearts, that every time she sees another innocent child at the First Communion rail, or another penitent sinner making his way to the Cross, or another broken heart pleading that the water of a wasted life be changed into the wine of God's love, she hears once again that word: "Woman, behold thy son."

The Consecration

My God, my God, why hast thou forsaken me?

—Matthew 27:46

The Fourth Word is the Consecration of the Mass of Calvary. We are now in the final stage of the Passion. In the fourth word, in all the universe, there is but God and Himself. This is the hour of darkness. Suddenly out of its blackness, the silence is broken by a cry—so terrible, so unforgettable, that even those who did not understand the dialect remembered the strange tones: "*Eli, Eli, lamma sabacthani.*" They recorded it so, a rough rendering of the Hebrew, because they could never get the sound of those tones out of their ears all the days of their lives.

The darkness that was covering the earth at that moment was only the external symbol of the dark night of the soul within. Well indeed might the sun hide its face at the terrible crime of Deicide. A real reason why the earth was made was to have a Cross erected upon it. And now that the Cross was erected, creation felt the pain and went into darkness.

But why the cry of darkness? Why the cry of abandonment: "My God, my God, why hast thou forsaken me?" It was the cry of atonement for sin. Sin is the abandonment of God by man; it is the creature forsaking the Creator, as a flower might abandon the sunlight, which gave its strength

51

and beauty. Sin is a separation, a divorce—the original divorce from unity with God, whence all other divorces are derived.

Since He came on earth to redeem men from sin, it was therefore fitting that He *feels* that abandonment, that separation, that divorce. He felt it first internally, in His soul, as the base of a mountain, if conscious, might feel abandoned by the sun when a cloud drifted about it, even though its great heights were radiant with light. There was no sin in His soul, but since He willed to feel the effect of sin, an awful sense of isolation and loneliness crept over Him—the loneliness of being without God.

Surrendering the divine consolation that might have been His, He sank into an awful human aloneness, to atone for the solitariness of a soul that has lost God by sin; for the loneliness of the atheist, who says there is no God; for the isolation of the man who gives up his faith for things; and for the brokenheartedness of all sinners who are homesick without God. He even went so far as to redeem all those who will not trust, who in sorrow and misery curse and abandon God, crying out: "Why this death? Why should I lose my property? Why should I suffer?" He atoned for all these things by asking a why of God.

But in order to reveal better the intensity of that feeling of abandonment, He revealed it by an external sign. Because man had separated himself from God, He, in atonement, permitted His blood to be separated from His body. Sin had entered into the blood of man; and as if the sins of the world were upon Him, He drained the chalice of His body of His sacred blood. We can almost hear Him say: "Father, this is my body; this is my blood. They are being separated from one another as humanity has been separated from Thee. This is the consecration of my Cross."

What happened there on the Cross that day is happening now in the Mass, with this difference: On the Cross, the Savior was alone; in the Mass, He is with us. Our Lord is now in heaven at the right hand of the Father, making intercession for us. He, therefore, can never suffer again *in His human nature*. How, then, can the Mass be the reenactment of Calvary? How can Christ renew the Cross? He cannot suffer again in His human nature, which is in heaven enjoying beatitude, but He can suffer again in our human natures. He cannot renew Calvary in His *physical body*, but He can renew it in *His Mystical Body* — the Church. The Sacrifice of the Cross can be reenacted, provided we give Him our body and our blood, and give it to Him so completely that, as His own, He can offer Himself anew to His heavenly Father for the redemption of His Mystical Body, the Church.

So, the Christ goes out into the world, gathering up other human natures who are willing to be Christs. In order that our sacrifices, our sorrows, our Golgothas, our crucifixions, may not be isolated, disjointed, and unconnected, the Church collects them, harvests them, unifies them, coalesces them, masses them, and this massing of all our sacrifices of our individual human natures is united with the great Sacrifice of Christ on the Cross in the Mass.

When we assist at the Mass, we are not just individuals of the earth or solitary units but living parts of a great spiritual order in which the Infinite penetrates and enfolds the finite, the Eternal breaks into the temporal, and the Spiritual clothes itself in the garments of materiality. Nothing more solemn exists on the face of God's earth than the awe-inspiring moment of Consecration; for the Mass is not a prayer, nor a hymn, nor something said — it is a divine act with which we come in contact at a given moment of time.

An imperfect illustration may be drawn from the radio. The air is filled with symphonies and speech. We do not put the words or music there; but, if we choose, we may establish contact with them by tuning in our radio. And so with the Mass. It is a singular, unique divine act with which we come in contact each time it is re-presented and reenacted in the Mass.

When the die of a medal or coin is struck, the medal is the material, visible representation of a spiritual idea existing in the mind of the artist. Countless reproductions may be made from that original, as each new piece of metal is brought in contact with it, and impressed by it. Despite the multiplicity of coins made, the pattern is always the same. In like manner, in the Mass, the pattern — Christ's sacrifice on Calvary — is renewed on our altars as each human being is brought in contact with it at the moment of consecration; but the sacrifice is one and the same, despite the multiplicity of Masses. The Mass, then, is the communication of the Sacrifice of Calvary to us under the species of bread and wine.

We are on the altar under the appearances of bread and wine, for both are the sustenance of life; therefore, in giving that which gives us life, we are symbolically giving ourselves. Furthermore, wheat must "suffer" to become bread; grapes must pass through the winepress to become wine. Hence, both are representative of Christians, who are called to suffer with Christ, that they may also reign with Him.

As the Consecration of the Mass draws near, Our Lord is equivalently saying to us: "You, Mary; you, John; you, Peter; and you, Andrew—you, all of you—give me your body; give me your blood. Give me your whole self! I can suffer no more. I have passed through my Cross, I have filled up the sufferings of my physical body, but I have not filled up the sufferings wanting to my Mystical Body, in which you are. The Mass is the moment when each one of you may literally fulfill my injunction: 'Take up your cross and follow me.'"

On the Cross, our Blessed Lord was looking forward to you, hoping that one day you would be giving yourself to Him at the moment of consecration. Today, in the Mass, that hope our Blessed Lord entertained for you is fulfilled. When you assist at the Mass, He expects you now to give Him yourself.

Then as the moment of consecration arrives, the priest, in obedience to the words of Our Lord, "Do this for a commemoration of me," takes bread in his hands and says, "This is my body"; and then over the chalice of wine says, "This is the chalice of my blood of the new and eternal testament." He does not consecrate the bread and wine together, but separately. The separate consecration of the bread and the wine is a symbolic representation of the separation of body and blood, and since the Crucifixion entailed that very mystery, Calvary is thus renewed on our altar. But Christ, as has been said, is not alone on our altar; we are with Him. Hence, the words of consecration have a double sense; the primary signification of the words is: "This is the Body of Christ; this is the Blood of Christ"; but the secondary signification is "This is my body; this is my blood."

Such is the purpose of life! To redeem ourselves in union with Christ; to apply His merits to our souls by being like Him in all things, even to His death on the Cross. He passed through His consecration on the Cross that we might now pass through ours in the Mass. There is nothing more tragic in all the world than wasted pain.

Think of how much suffering there is in hospitals and among the poor and the bereaved. Think also of how much of that suffering goes to waste! How many of those lonesome, suffering, abandoned, crucified souls are saying with Our Lord at the moment of consecration, "This is my body. Take it." And yet that is what we all should be saying at that second:

> I give myself to God. Here is my body. Take it. Here is my blood. Take it. Here is my soul, my will, my energy, my strength, my property, my wealth—all that I have. It is Yours. Take it! Consecrate it! Offer it! Offer it with Thyself to the heavenly Father, in order that He, looking down on this great sacrifice, may see only Thee, His beloved Son, in whom He is well pleased. Transmute the poor bread of my life into Thy divine life; thrill the wine of my wasted life into Thy divine spirit; unite my broken heart with Thy heart; change my cross into a crucifix. Let not my abandonment and my sorrow and my bereavement go to waste. Gather up the fragments, and as the drop of water is absorbed by the wine at the Offertory of the Mass, let my life be absorbed in Thine; let my little cross be entwined with Thy great Cross, so that I may purchase the joys of everlasting happiness in union with Thee.
>
> Consecrate these trials of my life, which would go unrewarded unless united with Thee; transubstantiate me so that, like bread, which is now Thy Body, and wine, which is now Thy Blood, I too may be wholly thine. I care not if the species remain, or that, like the bread and the wine, I seem to all earthly eyes the same as before. My station in life, my routine duties, my work, my

family—all these are but the species of my life, which may remain unchanged; but the *substance* of my life, my soul, my mind, my will, my heart—transubstantiate them, transform them wholly into Thy service, so that, through me, all may know how sweet is the love of Christ. Amen.

The Communion

I thirst.

—John 19:28

Our Blessed Lord reaches the Communion of His Mass when, out of the depths of the Sacred Heart, there wells the cry "I thirst." This was certainly not a thirst for water, for the earth is His and the fullness thereof; it was not a thirst for any of the refreshing draughts of earth, for He calmed the seas when they burst forth in their fury. When they offered Him a drink, He took it not. It was another kind of thirst that tortured Him. He was thirsty for the souls and hearts of men.

The cry was a cry for communion — the last in a long series of shepherding calls in the quest of God for men. The very fact that it was expressed in the most poignant of all human sufferings — namely, thirst — was the measure of its depth and intensity. Men may *hunger* for God, but God *thirsts* for men. He thirsted for man in Creation as He called him to fellowship with divinity in the garden of paradise; He thirsted for man in Revelation, as He tried to win back man's erring heart by telling the secrets of His love; He thirsted for man in the Incarnation, when He became like the one He loved and was found in the form and habit of man.

Now He was thirsting for man in Redemption, for greater love than this no man hath, that he lay down his life for his friends. It was the final appeal for communion before the curtain rang down on the great drama of His earthly life. All the myriad loves of parents for children, of spouse for spouse, if compacted into one great love, would have been the smallest fraction of God's love for man in that cry of thirst. It signified at once not only how much He thirsted for the little ones, for hungry hearts and empty souls, but also how intense was His desire to satisfy our deepest longing.

Really, there should be nothing mysterious in our thirst for God, for does not the hart pant after the fountain, and the sunflower turn to the sun and the rivers run into the sea? But that He should love us, considering our unworthiness, and how little our love is worth — *that is the mystery!* And yet such is the meaning of God's thirst for communion with us.

He had already expressed it in the parable of the lost sheep when He said He was not satisfied with the ninety-nine; only the lost sheep could give Him perfect joy. Now the truth was expressed again from the Cross: nothing could adequately satisfy His thirst, but the heart of every man, woman, and child, who were made for Him, and therefore could never be happy until they found their rest in Him.

The basis of this plea for communion is love, for love by its very nature tends to unity. Love of citizens for one another begets the unity of the state. Love of man and woman begets the unity of two in one flesh. The love of God for man, therefore, calls for a unity based upon the Incarnation — namely, the unity of all men in the Body and Blood of Christ.

In order, therefore, that God might seal His love for us, He gave us to Himself in Holy Communion, so that as He and His human nature, taken from the Blessed Mother, were one in the unity of His Person, so He and we taken, from the womb of humanity, might be one in the unity of the Mystical Body of Christ. Hence, we use the word *receive* when speaking of communion with Our Lord in the Eucharist, for literally we do *receive* divine life, just as really and truly as a babe receives the life of his mother.

All life is sustained by communion with a higher life. If the plants could speak, they would say to the moisture and the sunlight, "Unless you enter into communion with me, become possessed of my higher laws and powers, you shall not have life in you."

If the animals could speak, they would say to the plants: "Unless you enter into communion with me, you shall not have my higher life in you." We say to all lower creation: "Unless you enter into communion with me, you shall not share in my human life."

Why, then, should not Our Lord say to us: "Unless you enter into communion with me, you shall not have life in you"? The lower is transformed into, the higher, plants into animals, animals into man, and man, in a more exalted way, becomes "divinized" (if I may use that expression), through and through by the life of Christ.

Communion, then, is, first of all, the receiving of divine life, a life to which we are no more entitled than marble is entitled to bloom. It is a pure gift of an all-merciful, God who so loved us that He willed to be united with us, not in the bonds of flesh, but in the ineffable bonds of the Spirit, where love knows no satiety, but only rapture and joy.

And oh, how quickly we should have forgotten Him if we could not, like Bethlehem and Nazareth, receive Him into our souls! Neither gifts nor portraits take the place of the beloved one. And Our Lord knew it well. We needed Him, and so He gave us Himself.

But there is another aspect of Communion of which we but rarely think. Communion implies not only *receiving* divine life; it means also God *giving* human life. All love is reciprocal. There is no one-sided love, for love by its nature demands mutuality. God thirsts for us, but that means that man must also thirst for God. But do we ever think of Christ receiving Communion from us? Every time we go to the Communion rail, we say we "receive" Communion, and that is all many of us do, just "receive Communion."

There is another aspect of Communion besides receiving divine life, of which St. John speaks. St. Paul gives us the complementary truth in his First Letter to the Corinthians. Communion is not only an incorporation into the *life* of Christ; it is also an incorporation into His *death*. "As often as you shall eat this bread, and drink the chalice, you shall show the death of the Lord, until He come" (11:26).

Natural life has two sides: the anabolic and the catabolic. The supernatural also has two sides: the building up of the Christ pattern and the tearing down of the old Adam. Communion, therefore, implies not only a receiving but also a giving. There can be no ascent to a higher life without death to a lower one. Does not an Easter Sunday presuppose a Good Friday? Does not all love imply mutual self-giving, which ends in self-recovery?

This being so, should not the Communion rail be a place of exchange, instead of a place of exclusive receiving? Is all the *life* to pass from Christ to us and nothing to go back in return? Are we to drain the chalice and contribute nothing to its filling? Are we to receive the bread without giving wheat to be ground, to receive the wine and give no grapes to be crushed? If all we did during our lives was to go to Communion to receive divine life, to take it away and leave nothing behind, we would be parasites on the Mystical Body of Christ.

The Pauline injunction bids us fill up in our body the sufferings wanting to the Passion of Christ (Col. 1:24). We must therefore bring a spirit of sacrifice to the Eucharistic table; we must bring the mortification of our lower selves, the crosses patiently borne, the crucifixion of our egotism, the death of our concupiscence, and even the very difficulty of our coming to Communion. Then does Communion become what it was always intended to be—namely, a commerce between Christ and the soul, in which we give His death shown forth in our lives, and He gives His Life shown forth in our adopted sonship. We give Him our time; He gives us His eternity. We give Him our humanity; He gives us His divinity. We give Him our nothingness; He gives us His all.

Do we really understand the nature of love? Have we not sometimes, in great moments of affection for a little child, said in language that might vary from this, but which expresses the idea, "I love that child so much, I should just like to possess it within myself?" Why? Because all love craves unity. In the natural order, God has given great pleasures to the unity of the flesh. But those are nothing compared with the pleasure of the unity of the spirit when divinity passes out to humanity, and humanity to divinity — when our will goes to Him, and He comes to us so that we cease to be men and begin to be children of God.

If there has ever been a moment in your life when a fine, noble affection made you feel as if you had been lifted into the third or the seventh heaven; if there has ever been a time in your life when a noble love of a fine human heart cast you into an ecstasy; if there has ever been a time when you have really loved a human heart — then, I ask you, think of what it must be to be united with the great Heart of Love! If the human heart, in all its fine, noble, Christian riches, can so thrill, can so exalt, can make us so ecstatic, then what must be the great heart of Christ? Oh, if the spark is so bright, what must be the flame!

Do we fully realize how much Communion is bound up with sacrifice, both on the part of Our Lord and on the part of us, His poor weak creatures? The Mass makes the two inseparable: there is no Communion without a Consecration. There is no receiving the bread and wine we offer until they have been transubstantiated into the Body and Blood of Christ. Communion is the consequence of Calvary: we live by what we slay. All nature witnesses this truth; our bodies live by the slaying of the beasts of the fields and the plants of the gardens. We draw life from their crucifixion. We slay them not to destroy, but to fulfill; we immolate them for the sake of communion.

And now, by a beautiful paradox of divine love, God makes His Cross the very means of our salvation. We have slain Him; we nailed Him there; we crucified Him, but Love in His eternal Heart willed not to be defeated. He willed to give us the very life we slew; to give us the very Food we destroyed; to nourish us with the very Bread we buried and the very Blood we poured forth. He made our very crime a *happy fault*; He turned a Crucifixion into a Redemption; a Consecration into a Communion; a death into life everlasting.

And it is just that which makes man all the more mysterious! Why man should be loved is no mystery, but why he does not love in return is the great mystery. Why should Our Lord be the Great Unloved; why should Love not be loved? Why then, whenever He says, "I thirst," do we give Him vinegar and gall?

The Ite, Missa Est

It is finished.

—John 19:30

Our Blessed Savior now comes to the Ite, missa est of His Mass, as He utters the cry of triumph: "It is finished."

The work of salvation is finished, but when did it begin? It began back in the agelessness of eternity, when God willed to make man. Ever since the beginning of the world, there was a divine "impatience" to restore man to the arms of God.

The Word was impatient in heaven to be the "Lamb slain from the beginning of the world" (Rev. 13:8). He was impatient in prophetic types and symbols, as His dying face was reflected in a hundred mirrors stretching through all Old Testament history. He was impatient to be the real Isaac carrying the wood of His sacrifice in obedience to the commands of His heavenly Abraham. He was impatient to fulfill the mystical symbol of the Lamb of the Jewish Pasch, who was slain without a single bone of its body being broken. He was impatient to be the new Abel, slain by his jealous brethren of the race of Cain, that His blood might cry to Heaven for forgiveness. He was impatient in His mother's womb, as He saluted His precursor John. He was impatient in the Circumcision, as He anticipated His blood-shedding and received the name of "Savior."

He was impatient at the age of twelve, as He reminded His Mother that He had to be about His Father's business. He was impatient in His public life, as He said He had a baptism wherewith He was to be baptized, and He was "straitened until it be accomplished" (Luke 12:50). He was impatient in the Garden, as He turned His back to the consoling twelve legions of angels, to crimson olive roots with His redemptive Blood. He was impatient at His Last Supper, as He anticipated the separation of His Body and Blood under the appearance of bread and wine. And then, impatience closed as the hour of darkness drew near at the end of that Last Supper—He sang.

It was a trivial matter for the world if the stars burned brightly, or the mountains stood as symbols of perplexity, or the hills made their tribute to valleys, which gave them birth. What was important was that every single word predicted of Him should be true. Heaven and earth would not pass away until every jot and tittle had been fulfilled. There was only a little iota remaining, one tiny little jot; it was David's word about every prediction being fulfilled. Now that all else was fulfilled, He fulfilled that iota; He, the true David, quoted the prophetic David: "It is finished."

What is finished? The Redemption of man is finished. Love had completed its mission, for Love had done all that it could. There are two things Love can do. Love by its very nature tends to an Incarnation, and every Incarnation tends to a Crucifixion. Does not all true love tend toward an Incarnation? In the order of human love, does not the affection of husband for wife create from their mutual loves the incarnation of their confluent love in the form of a child? Once they have begotten their child, do not they make sacrifices for him, even to the point of death? And thus their love tends to a crucifixion.

But this is just a reflection of the divine order, where the love of God for man was so deep and intense that it ended in an Incarnation, which found God in the form and habit of man, whom He loved. But Our Lord's love for man did not stop with the Incarnation. Unlike everyone else who was ever born, Our Lord came into this world to redeem it. Death was the supreme goal He was seeking. Death interrupted the careers of great men, but it was no interruption to Our Lord; it was His crowning glory; it was the unique goal He was seeking.

His Incarnation thus tended to the Crucifixion, for "greater love than this no man has, that he lay down his life for his friends" (John 15:13). Now that Love had run its course in the Redemption of man, Divine Love could say: "I have done all for my vineyard that I can do" (see Isa. 5:4). Love can do no more than die. It is finished: "Ite, missa est."

His work is finished. But is ours? When He said, "It is finished," He did not mean that the opportunities of His life had ended; He meant that His work was done so perfectly that nothing could be added to it to make it more perfect—but with us, how seldom that is true. Too many of us end our lives, but few of us see them *finished.* A sinful life may end, but a sinful life is never a finished life.

If our lives just "end," our friends will ask: "How much did he leave?" But if our lives are "finished," our friends will ask: "How much did he take with him?" A finished life is not measured by years but by deeds; not by the time spent in the vineyard, but by the work done. In a short time, a man may fulfill many years; even those who come at the eleventh hour may finish their lives; even those who come to God like the thief at the last breath may finish their lives in the kingdom of God. Not for them the sad word of regret: "Too late, O ancient Beauty, have I loved Thee."[7]

Our Lord finished His work, but we have not finished ours. He pointed the way we must follow. He laid down the Cross at the finish, but we must take it up. He finished Redemption in His physical Body, but we have not finished it in His Mystical Body. He has finished salvation; we have not yet applied it to our souls. He has finished the Temple, but we must live in it. He has finished the model Cross; we must fashion ours to its pattern. He has finished sowing the seed; we must reap the harvest. He has finished filling the chalice, but we have not finished drinking its refreshing draughts. He has planted the wheat field; we

---

[7] St. Augustine, *Confessions,* bk. 10.

must gather it into our barns. He has finished the Sacrifice of Calvary; we must finish the Mass.

The Crucifixion was not meant to be an inspirational drama, but a pattern act on which to model our lives. We are not meant to sit and watch the Cross as something done and ended, like the life of Socrates. What was done on Calvary avails for us only in the degree that we repeat it in our own lives.

The Mass makes this possible, for at the renewal of Calvary on our altars, we are not onlookers but sharers in Redemption, and there it is that we "finish" our work. He has told us: "And I, if I be lifted up from the earth, will draw all things to myself" (John 12:32). He finished His work when He was lifted up on the Cross; we finish ours when we permit Him to draw us unto Himself in the Mass.

The Mass is that which makes the Cross visible to every eye; it placards the Cross at all the crossroads of civilization; it brings Calvary so close that even tired feet can make the journey to its sweet embrace; every hand may now reach out to touch its Sacred Burden, and every ear may hear its sweet appeal, for the Mass and the Cross are the same. In both, there is the same offering of a perfectly surrendered will of the beloved Son, the same body broken, the same blood flowed forth, the same divine forgiveness. All that has been said and done and acted during Holy Mass is to be taken away with us, lived, practiced, and woven into all the circumstances and conditions of our daily lives. His sacrifice is made our sacrifice by making it the oblation of ourselves in union with Him; His life given for us becomes our life given for Him. Thus do we return from Mass as those who have made their choice, turned their backs upon the world, and become other Christs for the generation in which we live — living potent witnesses to the Love that died that we might live with Love.

This world of ours is full of half-completed Gothic cathedrals, of half-finished lives and half-crucified souls. Some carry the Cross to Calvary and then abandon it; others are nailed to it and detach themselves before the elevation; others are crucified, but in answer to the challenge of the world "Come down," they come down after one hour, after two hours, after two hours and fifty-nine minutes. Real Christians are they who persevere unto the end. Our Lord stayed until He had finished.

The priest must likewise stay at the altar until the Mass is finished. He may not come down. So we must stay with the Cross until our lives are finished. Christ on the Cross is the pattern and model of a finished life. Our human nature is the raw material; our will is the chisel; God's grace is the energy and the inspiration.

Touching the chisel to our unfinished nature, we first cut off huge chunks of selfishness. Then, by more delicate chiselings, we dig away smaller bits of egotism until finally only a brush of the hand is needed to bring out the completed masterpiece—a finished man made to the image and likeness of the pattern on the Cross. We are at the altar under the symbol of bread and wine; we have offered ourselves to Our Lord; He has consecrated us.

We must therefore not take ourselves back, but remain there unto the end, praying unceasingly, that when the lease of our life has ended, and we look back upon a life lived in intimacy with the Cross, the echo of the Sixth Word may ring out on our lips: "It is finished."

And as the sweet accents of that "Ite, missa est" reach beyond the corridors of time and pierce the "hid battlements of Eternity,"[8] the angel choirs and the white-robed army of the Church Triumphant will answer back: "Deo gratias."

---

[8] Francis Thompson, "The Hound of Heaven," line 145.

The Last Gospel

Father, into thy hands, I commend my spirit.

—Luke 23:46

It is a beautiful paradox that the Last Gospel of the Mass takes us back to the beginning, for it opens with the words "In the beginning." And such is life: the last of this life is the beginning of the next. Fittingly indeed, then, the Last Word of Our Lord was His Last Gospel: "Father, into thy hands, I commend my spirit." Like the Last Gospel of the Mass, it, too, takes Him back to the beginning, for He now goes back to the Father, whence He came. He has completed His work. He began His Mass with the word *Father*. And He ends it with the same word.

"Everything perfect," the Greeks would say, "travels in circles." Just as the great planets, only after a long period of time, complete their orbits and then go back again to their starting points, as if to salute Him who sent them on their way, so the Word Incarnate, who came down to say His Mass, now completes His earthly career and goes back again to His heavenly Father, who sent Him on the journey of the world's redemption. The Prodigal Son is about to return to His Father's House, for is He not the Prodigal Son? Thirty-three years ago, He left the Father's house and the blessedness of heaven and came down to this earth of ours, which is a foreign country—for every country is foreign that is away from the Father's House.

For thirty-three years, He had been spending His substance. He spent the substance of His truth in the infallibility of His Church; He spent the substance of His power in the authority He gave to His Apostles and their successors. He spent the substance of His life in the Redemption and the sacraments. Now that every drop of it is gone, He looks longingly back again to the Father's house, and, with a loud cry, throws His spirit into His Father's arms, not in the attitude of one who is taking a plunge into the darkness, but as one who knows where He is going — to a homecoming with His Father.

In that Last Word and Last Gospel, which took Him back to the beginning of all beginnings — namely, His Father — is revealed the history and rhythm of life. The end of all things must, in some way, get back to the beginning. As the Son goes back to the Father; as Nicodemus must be born again; as the body returns to the dust — so the soul of man, which came from God, must one day go back to God.

Death is not the end of all. The cold clod falling upon the grave does not mark finis to the history of a man. The way he has lived in this life determines how he shall live in the next. If he has sought God during life, death will be like the opening of a cage, enabling him to use his wings to fly to the arms of the Divine Beloved. If he has fled from God during life, death will be the beginning of an eternal flight away from Life and Truth and Love — and that is hell.

Before the throne of God, whence we came on our earthly novitiate, we must one day go back to render an account of our stewardship. There will not be a human creature who, when the last sheaf is garnered, will not be found either to have accepted or rejected the divine gift of Redemption and, in accepting or rejecting it, to have signed the warrant of his eternal destiny.

As the sales on a cash register are recorded for the end of our business day, so our thoughts, words, and deeds are recorded for the Final Judgment. If we but live in the shadow of the Cross, death will not be an ending but a beginning of eternal life. Instead of a parting, it will be a meeting; instead of a going away, it will be an arriving; instead of being an end, it will be a Last Gospel — a return to the beginning. As a voice whispers, "You must leave the earth," the Father's voice will say, "My child, come unto me."

We have been sent into this world as children of God, to assist at the Holy Sacrifice of the Mass. We are to take our stand at the foot of the Cross and, like those who stood under it the first day, we will be asked to declare our loyalties. God has given us the wheat and the grapes of life, and as the men who, in the Gospel, were given talents, we will have to show return on that divine gift.

God has given us our lives as wheat and grapes. It is our duty to consecrate them and bring them back to God as bread and wine—transubstantiated, divinized, and spiritualized. There must be harvest in our hands after the springtime of the earthly pilgrimage.

That is why Calvary is erected in the midst of us, and we are on its sacred hill. We were not made to be mere onlookers, shaking our dice like the executioners of old, but rather, to be participants in the mystery of the Cross.

If there is any way to picture judgment in terms of the Mass, it is to picture it in the way the Father greeted His Son—namely, by looking at His hands. They bore the marks of labor, the callouses of redemption, and the scars of salvation. So too, when our earthly pilgrimage is over, and we go back to the beginning, God will look at both of our hands. If our hands in life touched the hands of His Divine Son, they will bear the same livid marks of nails; if our feet in life have trodden over the same road that leads to eternal glory through the detour of a rocky and thorny Calvary, they shall bear the same bruises; if our hearts beat in unison with His, they shall show the riven side that the wicked lance of jealous earth did pierce.

Blessed indeed are they who carry in their cross-marked hands the bread and wine of consecrated lives signed with the sign and sealed with the seal of redemptive Love. But woe unto them who come from Calvary with hands unscarred and white.

God grant that when life is over, and the earth is vanishing like a dream of one awakening when eternity is flooding our souls with its splendors, we may, with humble and triumphant faith, echo the Last Word of Christ: "Father, into thy hands I commend my spirit."

And so the Mass of Christ ends. The Confiteor was His prayer to the Father for the forgiveness of our sins; the Offertory was the presentation on the paten of the Cross of small hosts of the thief and ourselves; the Sanctus was His commending us to Mary, the Queen of Saints; the Consecration was the separation of His blood from His body, and the seeming separation of divinity and humanity; the Communion was His thirst for the souls of men; the Ite, missa est was the finishing of the work of salvation; the Last Gospel was the return to the Father, whence He came.

And now that the Mass is over, and He has commended His Spirit to the Father, He prepares to give back His body to His Blessed Mother at the foot of the Cross. Thus will the end be the beginning, for at the beginning of His earthly life, He was nestled on her lap in Bethlehem, and now, on Calvary, He will take His place there once again.

Earth had been cruel to Him; His feet wandered after lost sheep, and we dug them with steel; His hands stretched out the bread of everlasting life, and we fastened them with nails; His lips spoke the truth, and we sealed them with dust. He came to give us life, and we took away His. But that was our fatal mistake. We really did not take it away. We only tried to take it away. He laid it down of Himself. Nowhere do the Evangelists say that He died. They say, "He gave up the spirit." It was a willing, self-determined relinquishment of life.

It was not death that approached Him; it was He who approached death. That is why, as the end draws near, the Savior commands the portal of death to open unto Him in the presence of the Father. The chalice is gradually being drained of its rich red wine of salvation. The rocks of earth open their hungry mouths to drink, as if more thirsty for the draughts of salvation than the parched hearts of men; the earth itself shook in horror because men had erected God's Cross upon its breast. Magdalene, the penitent, as usual, clings to His feet, and there she will be again on Easter morn; John, the priest, with a face like a cast molded out of love, listens to the beating of the Heart whose secrets He learned and loved and mastered; Mary thinks how different Calvary is from Bethlehem.

Thirty-three years ago, Mary looked down at His sacred face; now He looks down at her. In Bethlehem, heaven looked up into the face of earth; now, the roles are reversed. Earth looks up into the face of heaven—but a heaven marred by the scars of earth. He loved her above all the creatures of earth, for she was His Mother and the Mother of us all. He saw her first on coming to earth; He shall see her last on leaving it. Their eyes meet, all aglow with life, speaking a language all their own. There is a rupture of a heart through a rapture of love, then a bowed head, a broken heart. Back to the hands of God, He gives, pure and sinless, His spirit, in loud and ringing voice that trumpets eternal victory. And Mary stands alone a Childless Mother. Jesus is dead!

Mary looks up into His eyes, which are so clear even in the face of death:

High Priest of Heaven and earth, Thy Mass is finished! Leave the altar of the Cross and repair into Thy Sacristy. As High Priest Thou didst come forth from the sacristy of Heaven, panoplied in the vestments of humanity and bearing Thy Body as Bread and Thy Blood as Wine.

Now the Sacrifice has been consummated. The Consecration bell has rung. Thou didst offer Thy Spirit to Thy Father; Thy Body and Thy Blood to man. There remains now nothing but the drained chalice. Enter into Thy sacristy. Take off the garments of mortality and put on the white robes of immortality. Show Thy hands, and feet, and side to Thy heavenly Father and say: "With these was I wounded in the house of those that love me."

Enter, High Priest, into Thy heavenly sacristy, and as Thy earthly ambassadors hold aloft the Bread and Wine, do Thou show Thyself to the Father in loving intercession for us even unto the consummation of the world. Earth has been cruel to Thee, but Thou wilt be kind to earth. Earth lifted Thee on the Cross, but now Thou shalt lift earth unto the Cross. Open the door of the heavenly Sacristy, O High Priest! Behold, it is now we who stand at the door and knock!

And Mary, what shall we say to Thee? Thou art the sacristan of the High Priest! Thou wert a sacristan in Bethlehem when He did come to Thee as wheat and grapes in the crib of Bethlehem. Thou wert His sacristan at the Cross, where He became the Living Bread and Wine through the Crucifixion. Thou art His sacristan now, as He comes from the altar of the Cross wearing only the drained chalice of His sacred Body.

As that chalice is laid in your lap, it may seem that Bethlehem has come back again, for He is once more yours. But it only seems—for in Bethlehem, He was the chalice whose gold was to be tried by fire, but now at Calvary, He is the chalice whose gold has passed through the fires of Golgotha and Calvary. In Bethlehem He was white as He came from the Father: now He is red as He came from us. But thou art still His sacristan! And as the Immaculate Mother of all hosts who go to the altar, do thou, O Virgin Mary, send us there pure, and keep us pure, even unto the day when we enter into the heavenly sacristy of the kingdom of heaven, where thou wilt be our eternal sacristan and He our eternal Priest."

And you, friends of the Crucified, your High Priest has left the Cross, but He has left us the altar. On the, Cross He was alone; in the Mass, He is with us. On the Cross, He suffered in His physical Body; on the altar, He suffers in the Mystical Body, which we are. On the Cross, He was the unique Host; in the Mass, we are the small hosts, and He the large host receiving His Calvary through us. On the Cross, He was the wine; in the Mass, we are the drop of water united with the wine and consecrated with Him. In that sense, He is still on the Cross, still saying the Confiteor with us, still forgiving us, still commending us to Mary, still thirsting for us, still drawing us unto the Father, for as long as sin remains on earth, still will the Cross remain.

Whenever there is silence around me
By day or by night —
I am startled by a cry.
It came down from the Cross.
The first time I heard it
I went out and searched —

And found a man in the throes of Crucifixion.

And I said: "I will take you down,"
And I tried to take the nails out of His Feet,

But He said: "Let them be, for I cannot be taken down
Until every man, every woman, and every child

Come together to take me down."
And I said: "But I cannot bear your cry. What can I do?"
And He said: "Go about the world —
Tell everyone that you meet —
There is a Man on the Cross."[9]

---

[9] Elizabeth Cheney, "There Is a Man on the Cross," stanza 1.

3

The Holy Hour:
Meditations and Reflections

"Could You Not Watch One Hour with Me?"

Why Make A Holy Hour?

The purpose of these meditations is to aid souls in securing an inner peace by meditating one continuous hour a day on God and our immortal destiny. Whether or not one uses these meditations does not matter in the least. Some Jews, some Protestants, and some Catholics may find it very unsatisfactory. If, however, they reject these because they wish to make the Holy Hour in their own way, they will have achieved its purpose. What is vital is not that these meditations be used, but that there be meditation.

But why spend an hour a day in meditation? Because we are living on the surface of our souls, knowing little either of God or our inner self. Our knowledge is mostly about things, not about destiny. Most of our difficulties and disappointments in life are due to mistakes in our life plans. Having forgotten the purpose of living, we have doubted even the value of living. A broken bone gives pain because it is not where it ought to be; our souls are in agony because we are not tending to the fullness of Life, Truth, and Love, which is God.

But why make a Holy Hour? Here are ten reasons.

1. It is time spent in the presence of Our Lord Himself. If faith is alive, no further reason is needed.

2. In our busy lives, it takes considerable time to shake off the "noonday devils," the worldly cares, that cling to our souls like dust. An hour with Our Lord follows the experience of the disciples on the road to Emmaus (Luke 24:13–35). We begin by walking with Our Lord, but our eyes are "held fast" so that we do not "recognize him." Next, He converses with our soul, as we read the Scriptures. The third stage is one of sweet intimacy, as when "he sat down at table with them." The fourth stage is the full dawning of the mystery of the Eucharist. Our eyes are "opened," and we recognize Him. Finally, we reach the point where we do not want to leave. The hour seemed so short. As we arise, we ask: "Were not our hearts burning within us when he spoke to us on the road, and when he made the Scriptures plain to us?" (Luke 24:32).

3. Our Lord asked for it. "Had you no strength, then, to watch with me even for an hour?" (see Matt. 26:40). The word was addressed to Peter, but he is referred to as Simon. It is our Simon nature that needs the hour. If the hour seems hard, it is because "the spirit is willing enough, but the flesh is weak" (Mark 14:38).

4. The Holy Hour keeps a balance between the spiritual and the practical. Western philosophies tend to an activism in which God does nothing, and man everything; the Eastern philosophies tend to a quietism in which God does everything, and man nothing. The golden mean is in the words of St. Thomas: "action following rest," Martha walking with Mary. The Holy Hour unites the contemplative to the active life of the person.

Thanks to the hour with Our Lord, our meditations and resolutions pass from the conscious to the subconscious and then become motives of action. A new spirit begins to pervade our work. The change is effected by Our Lord, who fills our heart and works through our hands. A person can give only what he possesses. To give Christ to others, one must possess Him.

5. The Holy Hour will make us practice what we preach. "Here is an image," he said, "of the kingdom of heaven: there was once a king, who

held a marriage feast for his son and sent out his servants with a summons to all those whom he had invited to the wedding; but they would not come" (Matt. 22:2–3).

It was written of Our Lord that He "began to do and to teach" (Acts 1:1). The person who practices the Holy Hour will find that when he teaches, the people will say of him as of the Lord: "All ... were astonished at the gracious words which came from his mouth" (Luke 4:22).

6. The Holy Hour helps us make reparation for the sins of the world and for our own sins. When the Sacred Heart appeared to St. Margaret Mary, it was His Heart, and not His head, that was crowned with thorns. It was Love that was hurt. Black Masses, sacrilegious communions, scandals, militant atheism—who will make up for them? Who will be an Abraham for Sodom, a Mary for those who have no wine? The sins of the world are our sins as if we had committed them. If they caused Our Lord a bloody sweat, to the point that He upbraided His disciples for failing to stay with Him an hour, shall we with Cain ask: "Is it for me to watch over my brother?" (Gen. 4:9).

7. It reduces our liability to temptation and weakness. Presenting ourselves before Our Lord in the Blessed Sacrament is like putting a tubercular patient in good air and sunlight. The virus of our sins cannot long exist in the face of the Light of the world. "Always I can keep the Lord within sight; always he is at my right hand, to make me stand firm" (Ps. 15:8).

Our sinful impulses are prevented from arising through the barrier erected each day by the Holy Hour. Our will becomes disposed to goodness with little conscious effort on our part. Satan, the roaring lion, was not permitted to put forth his hand to touch righteous Job until he received permission (Job 1:12). Certainly, then, will the Lord withhold serious fall from him who watches (1 Cor. 10:13). With full confidence in his Eucharistic Lord, the person will have a spiritual resiliency. He will bounce back quickly after a falling: "Fall I, it is but to rise again, sit I in darkness, the Lord will be my light. The Lord's displeasure I must bear, I that have sinned against him, till at last, he admits my plea, and grants redress" (Micah 7:8–9).

The Lord will be favorable even to the weakest of us, if He finds us at His feet in adoration, disposing ourselves to receive divine favors. No sooner had Saul of Tarsus, the persecutor, humbled himself before his Maker than God sent a special messenger to his relief, telling him that "even now he is at his prayers" (Acts 9:11). Even the person who has fallen can expect reassurance if he watches and prays. "They shall increase, that hitherto had dwindled, be exalted, that once were brought low" (Jer. 30:19).

8. The Holy Hour is a personal prayer. The person who limits himself strictly to his official obligation is like the union man who downs tools the moment the whistle blows. Love begins when duty finishes. It is a giving of the cloak when the coat is taken. It is walking the extra mile. "Answer shall come ere cry for help is uttered; prayer find audience while it is yet on their lips" (Isa. 65:24).

Of course, we do not have to make a Holy Hour — and that is just the point. Love is never compelled, except in hell. There love has to submit to justice. To be forced to love would be a kind of hell. No man who loves a woman is obligated to give her an engagement ring, and no person who loves the Sacred Heart ever has to give an engagement Hour.

"Would you, too, go away?" (John 6:68) is *weak* love; "Art thou sleeping?" (Mark 14:37) is *irresponsible* love; "He had great possessions" (Matt. 19:22; Mark 10:22) is *selfish* love. But does the person who loves His Lord have time for other activities before he performs acts of love "above and beyond the call of duty"? Does the patient love the physician who charges for every call, or does he begin to love when the physician says: "I just dropped by to see how you were"?

9. Meditation keeps us from seeking an external escape from our worries and miseries. When difficulties arise, when nerves are made taut by false accusations, there is always a danger that we may look outwards, as the Israelites did, for release.

From the Lord God, the Holy One of Israel, word was given you: "Come back and keep still, and all shall be well with you; in quietness and in confidence lies your strength. But you would have none of it; To horse! you cried, We must flee! and flee you shall; We must ride swiftly, you said, but swifter still ride your pursuers" (Isa. 30:15–16).

No outward escape, neither pleasure, drink, friends, or keeping busy, is an answer. The soul cannot "fly upon a horse"; he must take "wings" to a place where his "life is hidden away … with Christ in God" (Col. 3:3).

10. Finally, the Holy Hour is necessary for the Church. No one can read the Old Testament without becoming conscious of the presence of God in history. How often did God use other nations to punish Israel for her sins! He made Assyria the "rod that executes my vengeance" (Isa. 10:5). The history of the world since the Incarnation is the Way of the Cross. The rise of nations and their fall remain related to the kingdom of God. We cannot understand the mystery of God's government, for it is the "sealed book" of Revelation. John wept when he saw it (Rev. 5:4). He could not understand why this moment of prosperity and that hour of adversity.

The sole requirement is the venture of faith, and the reward is the depths of intimacy for those who cultivate His friendship. To abide with Christ is spiritual fellowship, as He insisted on the solemn and sacred night of the Last Supper, the moment He chose to give us the Eucharist: "You have only to live on in me, and I will live on in you" (John 15:4). He wants us in His dwelling: "That you, too, may be where I am" (John 14:3).

How to Make the Holy Hour (for Laity)

"Let nothing hinder thee from praying always, and be not afraid to be justified even to death for the rewards of God continue forever. Before prayer prepare thy soul; and be not as a man that tempt God" (Sir. 18:22–23, Douay-Rheims).

Prayer is the lifting of our soul to God unto the end of perfectly corresponding to His holy will. Our Divine Lord, describing His mission, said: "For I have come down from heaven, not to do my own will, but the will of him who sent me ... the Father, that I should lose nothing of what he has given me, but that I should raise it up on the last day" (see John 6:38–39). "My food is to do the will of him who sent me, to accomplish his work" (see John 4:34).

To correspond to the divine will, we must, first of all, know it, and secondly, have the grace and strength to correspond with it, once it is known. But to attain these two gifts of light for our minds and power for our wills, we must live on terms of intimate friendship with God. This is done through prayer. A prayerful life is, therefore, one lived in conformity with the holy will of God as a prayerless life is a life of self-will and selfishness.

There is an element of prayer common to Jews, Protestants, and Catholics—namely, belief in God. More than half of the prayers, for example, which a priest says in his Divine Office, are taken from the Old Testament. In relation to all three—that is, Jews, Protestants, and Catholics—a Holy Hour will, therefore, be understood as one hour a day spent in meditating on God and our eternal salvation. This Holy Hour can be made anywhere.

For Catholics, however, the Holy Hour has a very special significance. It means a continuous and unbroken hour spent in the presence of Our Divine Lord in the Eucharist; for which reason a meditation on the Blessed Eucharist has been included as one of these meditations in this book.

In the case of priests and religious, it is suggested that they make this Holy Hour in addition to their usual recitation of the Divine Office and Holy Mass.

This Holy Hour will be spent in prayer and meditation. A distinction is here made between the two, with the emphasis on the latter. By prayer, we here understand the recitation of formal prayers, generally composed by a person different from him who prays.

The psalms represent one of the highest forms of vocal prayer and are common to Jews, Protestants, and Catholics. Other vocal prayers include the Our Father, the Hail Mary, the Creed, the Confiteor, Acts of Faith, Hope, and Charity, and thousands of other prayers found in religious books. There are three kinds of attention in vocal prayer: (1) to the words, lest we say them wrong; (2) to their sense and meaning; and (3) to God and the intention for which we pray. The last kind of attention is essential to vocal prayer.

But the principal purpose of these Holy Hour meditations is the cultivation of mental prayer, or meditation. Very few souls ever meditate; they are either frightened by the word or else were never taught its existence. In the human order, a person in love is always conscious of the one loved, lives in the presence of the other, resolves to do the will of the other, and regards as his greatest jealousy being outdone in the least advantage of self-giving. Apply this to a soul in love with God, and you have the rudiments of meditation.

Meditation is, therefore, a kind of communing of spirit with spirit, with God as its object. Without attempting to set down the formal aspects of meditation, but to make it as intelligible as possible to beginners, the technique of meditation is as follows:

1. *We speak to God.* We begin by putting ourselves in the presence of God. For those who make the Holy Hour before the Blessed Sacrament, there must be a consciousness of our presence before the Body, Blood, Soul, and Divinity of Our Lord and Savior, Jesus Christ. Naturally, there are varying degrees of intimacy with persons. In a theater, there are hundreds present but little or no intimacy between them. The intimacy deepens to the degree that we establish conversation with one or more of them, and according as this conversation springs from a common interest. So it is with God.

Prayer, then, is not a mere asking for things, but an aiming at a transformation; that is, a becoming "conformed to the image of his Son" (Rom. 8:29, KJV). We pray not to dispose God to give us something, but to dispose ourselves to receive something from Him: the fullness of divine life.

2. *God speaks to us.* Activity is not only on the human side but also on the divine. A conversation is an exchange, not a monologue. As the soul wills to draw near God, God wills to draw near the soul. It would be wrong to monopolize a conversation with friends; it is more wrong to do so in our relations with God. We must not do all the talking; we must also be good listeners. "Speak, LORD, for thy servant heareth" (1 Kings [1 Sam.] 3:9, KJV).

The soul now experiences the truth of the words "Draw near to God, and he will draw near to you" (see James 4:8). All during the meditation, it will conceive devout affections of adoration, petition, sacrifice, and reparation to God, but particularly at the close of the meditation. These affections or colloquies are to be offered preferably in our own words, for every soul must love God in its own way, and God loves each soul in a particular manner.

In the beginning, the soul attracted to Jesus by some impulse of grace, comes to Him, filled with natural thoughts and aspirations, and very ignorant of the supernatural. It understands neither God nor itself. It has a few intimate relations with the Divinity outside of itself and within itself, but it begins to converse with Jesus. If it persists in the frequentation of His company, the Lord gradually takes an ever-increasing share in the conversation and begins to enlighten the soul. In its contemplation of the mysteries of faith, He aids it to penetrate beneath the words and facts and symbols, hitherto known but superficially, and to grasp the inner sense of the supernatural truths contained in these facts or words or symbols. The Scriptures are gradually opened to the soul. The well-known texts begin to acquire a new and deeper meaning. Familiar expressions convey a knowledge, which the soul wonders never to have before discovered in them. All this new light is directed towards giving a fuller and more perfect comprehension of the mysteries of our faith, which are the mysteries of the life of Jesus.[10]

Do not read these meditations as a story. Read a few lines slowly; close the book; think about the truth contained in them; apply them to your life; speak to God about how little you have corresponded to His will, how anxious you are to do it; listen to God speaking to your soul; make acts of faith, hope, and love to God; and only when that train of thought has been exhausted should you proceed to the next idea. A single Holy Hour will not necessarily require reading a chapter. If one meditates well, a single chapter should provide thoughts for many Holy Hours.

When these meditations are exhausted, take up either the Sacred Scriptures or some truly spiritual book, or the life of a saint, and use it for inspiration and for meditation.

How to Make the Holy Hour (for Priests)

If at all possible, the priest should make his daily Holy Hour before celebrating Mass. Now that the Church's regulations on the pre-Eucharistic fast have been modified, he will be well advised to take a cup of coffee before he starts. The average American is physically, biologically, psychologically, and neurologically unable to do anything worthwhile before he has a cup of coffee. And that goes for prayer, too. Even sisters in convents whose rules were written before electric percolators were developed, would do well to update their procedures. Let them have coffee before meditation.

Limit the saying of the Breviary to twenty minutes of the hour. The basic purpose of this hour is to meditate. Some spiritual writers recommend a mechanical division of the hour into four parts: thanksgiving, petition, adoration, and reparation. This is unnecessarily artificial. An

---

[10] Edward Leen, *Progress through Mental Prayer* (New York: Sheed and Ward, 1940), 29.

hour's conversation with a friend is not divided into four rigid segments or topics. The Holy Hour is not an official prayer; it is personal. Each priest, being a man, has a heart unlike any other in the world. This unique heart must make up the content of his prayer. God no more likes "circular letters" than we do. In addition to liturgical or official prayer, there must be the prayer of the heart. We constantly preach to others; in the Holy Hour, we preach to ourselves.

Many books on meditation have a rigid format that is endurable in the seminary, but which the priest soon finds too dry for his purposes. The so-called methods of meditation are generally impractical and unsuited to our mentality. What they consist in is an analysis of a meditation that was already made and proved satisfactory for the one who made it. A child will run after a ball with grace and freedom of movement. But if he is told to narrate what he does every second, how he first lifts his right foot, then his left, all the spontaneity disappears. To base a meditation, first on the intellect, then on the will, and finally on the emotions, is to destroy intimacy. This is not what really happens. The intellect does not work first in meditation, then the will, then the imagination. The person meditates; all his faculties work together. To achieve this, the greatest possible freedom should be left to the individual: "Where the Lord's Spirit is, there is freedom" (2 Cor. 3:17).

The best book for meditation is Scripture. But since many of its depths need to be explained, a good spiritual commentary is valuable. Too often the Lord may have to repeat the complaint He voiced to His disciples: "You do not understand the scriptures or what is the power of God" (Matt. 22:29).

Read the Scriptures, or a commentary, or any solid spiritual book, until a thought strikes you. Then close the book, and talk to Our Lord about it. But do not do all the talking. Listen also. "Speak on, Lord, thy servant is listening" (1 Kings [Sam.] 3:10) must not be: "Listen, Lord, thy servant speaketh." We learn to speak through listening, and we grow in love of God through listening. Meditation is at least half-listening: "It is my turn to ask questions" (Job 40:2).

When you are so fatigued and exhausted that you cannot pray, offer up your worthlessness. Does not a dog love to be near the master, even when the master gives him no evident sign of affection?

Allow no difficulty in making the Holy Hour to be an excuse for giving it up. When making it is a pleasure, we can think of ourselves as priests; when it is an effort, we can remember that we are also victims. Then we become like Moses, who asked God to blot his name from the record if this would win pardon for the people (Exod. 32:31–32), and like Paul, who was willing to be accursed for his race (Rom. 9:1–3). The very effort we put forth each day makes us masters of ourselves and, therefore, better servants of the Sacred Heart.

When tempted to give up the Hour, ask yourself which of these three excuses, which the Lord said (Luke 9:57–62) would be ours, are keeping us back from total service: earthly desires, earthly love, or earthly grief.

Sit or Kneel?

Should one kneel, sit, stand, or walk during the Holy Hour? Scripture records examples of each of these various attitudes. The publican who stood in the back of the Temple was accounted justified. St. Simplician, who succeeded St. Ambrose as bishop of Milan, asked Augustine what was the proper attitude to pray and why David did not kneel praying before the tabernacle. Augustine replied that one should adopt the bodily position best calculated to move the soul. Aristotle said that the soul, by sitting, becomes wise. St. Jerome's rule was that in praying and in meditating, the body should always take the position that seemed best for exciting the soul's internal devotion.

Sitting is sometimes associated with despair and weariness in Scripture. When Israel was brought into captivity, and Jerusalem left deserted, "the prophet Jeremiah sat down there and wept" (Lam. 1:1). Elias, too, in his despair, sat down under a juniper tree and "prayed to have done with life" (3 Kings [1 Kings] 19:4). The exiles from Jerusalem are pictured in the psalm: "We sat down by the streams of Babylon and wept there, remembering Sion" (Ps. 136 [137]:1). And when Moses was praying for victory against Amalek, his "arms grew weary; so they found him a stone to sit on and bade him be seated on it" (Exod. 17:12).

On the other hand, Our Blessed Lord prayed in the garden on His knees: "He fell upon his face in prayer" (Matt. 26:39). Stephen prayed in the same position: "Kneeling down, he cried, aloud, Lord, do not count this sin against them" (Acts 7:59). After the miraculous draught of fishes: "Simon Peter fell down and caught Jesus by the knees; Leave me to myself, Lord, I am a sinner" (Luke 5:8). St. Paul evidently prayed kneeling: "I fall on my knees to the Father of our Lord Jesus Christ" (Eph. 3:14). The young man who came to Our Lord inquiring what he must do to receive eternal life "knelt down before him" (Mark 10:17). Even when the soldiers mocked Our Blessed Lord, after beating Him over the head with a rod and spitting upon Him, they "bowed their knees in worship of him" (Mark 15:19). The gesture of ridicule is an obvious mockery of a gesture of worship.

When Our Lord went into the garden, He "knelt down to pray" (Luke 22:41). When Peter raised Tabitha from the dead, he "went on his knees to pray" (Acts 9:40). When Paul came to Ephesus and quoted the only words spoken by Our Lord recorded in Scripture other than in the Gospels ("It is more blessed to give than to receive"), he "knelt down and prayed with them all" (Acts 20:35–36). The psalmist used a like expression: "Come in, then, fall we down in worship, bowing the knee before God who made us" (94:6). The mother of the sons of Zebedee adopted the same position when seeking preferment for her two boys, "falling on her knees to make a request of him" (Matt. 20:20).

The father who had the lunatic son came to Our Lord "and knelt before him: Lord, he said, have pity on my son, who is a lunatic" (Matt. 17:14). The leper who came up to Our Blessed Lord in the synagogue in Galilee to be healed knelt at His feet and said, "If it be thy will, thou hast power to make me clean" (Mark 1:40). The condition that the devil imposed upon Our Blessed Lord for giving Him all the kingdoms of the world was likewise that of kneeling: "If thou wilt fall down before me and worship" (Luke 4:7). Peter, on the contrary, was standing when he warmed himself by the fire (John 18:18, 25).

The conclusion is obvious. It is best to kneel during the Hour, for it indicates humility, follows the example of Our Lord in the garden, makes atonement for our failings, and is a polite gesture before the King of Kings.

How Often?

Should the priest, who hears the appeal of the suffering Savior to watch an Hour with Him, make the sacrifice once a week? No! It is too hard. What is done once a week, is an interruption of our normal life. The temptation is to put it off until the end of the week, thereby running the risk of not doing it at all.

The weekly Holy Hour can never become a habit. Once a week is not a deep token of love. What mother is content to see her child once a week; what wife her husband? Love is not intermittent. Medicines taken once a week can give little strength.

If the Holy Hour once a week is too difficult, how often should it be made? The answer is obvious. It should be made every day.

The Holy Hour made once a week is an interruption to the week. But made daily, its absence is an interruption. Furthermore, an act that becomes a habit by daily repetition loses its difficulty. What at first was imperfectly performed, by habit becomes easier with each progressive stroke. If the Holy Hour is repeated daily at the same hour, we start it without premeditation; it becomes almost automatic. The daily Holy Hour becomes as easy as anything we do daily. It becomes not just a habit but part of a priest's nature. As Aristotle wrote in his *Rhetoric*:

> That which has become habitual becomes, as it were, a part of our nature; habit is something like nature, for the difference between "often" and "always" is not great, and nature belongs to the idea of "always," habit to that of "often."

In the Old Testament, the manna fell each day, not just weekly. "But the Lord said to Moses, 'I mean to rain down bread upon you from heaven. It will be for the people to go out and gather enough for their needs, day by day; and so I shall have a test, whether they are ready to follow my orders or not'" (Exod. 16:4)

God promised to give them bread every day, but on the day before the Sabbath, there fell a double supply, for none would fall on the Sabbath. This daily gathering was a test of love and obedience. The Lord always has a test: in the desert, as well as in the garden. The first parents were tested by the prohibition to eat the fruit of the tree of the knowledge of good and evil. The obedience of the Israelites was tested by the command not to gather on ordinary days more than enough for that day. All life is a probation. The inference suggested is that under the new dispensation, a daily faith in the Eucharist by a Holy Hour is a proof of our faithfulness.

The manna taught a daily lesson of dependence on God, and it played an important part in the spiritual education of Israel. It came not by fits or in starts, but in a regular way. What the Lord gave daily, we can return daily.

The priest should think of the practice of the daily Holy Hour as something to continue for his whole life. The children of Israel ate the manna for forty years (Exod. 16:35), until they came to the borders of the land of Canaan. The forty years represent the pilgrimage of life. It spiritually implies that every priest should daily gather heavenly manna for his soul.

The daily Holy Hour gives us wisdom. Daily adoration of the Eucharist was implied not only in the type or prefigurement of the manna, but also in the way wisdom is given to those who fulfill the indicated conditions. Our Lord said that those who did His will would know His doctrine. This means that knowledge is necessary in the beginning in order to love, but that later love deepens knowledge. The book of Proverbs, speaking of the wisdom that is older than this world, summons the soul to an early and a daily watching: "Love me, and thou shalt earn my love; wait early at my doors, and thou shalt gain access to me" (Prov. 8:17).

The mind of the priest who lives close to the tabernacle door gains a special illumination. The priest's mind and heart are best guided when they seek the Eucharistic Lord at dawn. The young priest, too, is strengthened who begins his watch at the tabernacle door in the first days of his priesthood.

Another passage in the book of Proverbs describing the daily search for wisdom at the feet of the Lord is frequently applied to the Blessed Mother: "I was at his side, a master-workman my delight increasing with each day, as I made play before him all the while; made play in this world of dust, with the sons of Adam for my play-fellows" (Prov. 8:30–31).

It is certainly worthy to note that this delight is described not as spasmodic or hebdomadal, but day by day. "Blessed are they who listen to me, keep vigil, day by day, at my threshold, watching till I open my doors" (Prov. 8:34).

Daily exigencies demand a daily Holy Hour. The Lord's Prayer reminds us that yesterday's food does not nourish us today: "Give us this day our daily bread" (Matt. 6:11).

Vitamins cannot be stored up. Spiritual energy has to be renewed; today's strength must come from the Lord today. Thus, the monotony of life is broken, and there comes to the priest new power for each day's apostolate. The Holy Hour each day also destroys in the priest forebodings and worries about the future. Kneeling before the Eucharistic Lord, he receives the rations for each day's march, worrying not at all about the morrow.

The Holy Hour should be a daily event because our crosses are daily, not weekly. "If any man has a mind to come my way, let him renounce self, and take up his cross daily, and follow me" (Luke 9:23).

Our children, our missions, our debts, our ulcers, our pet peeves—none of them come in octaves. Their horizontal and vertical weavings form for us a daily cross. These daily crosses will sour us, sear our souls, and make us bitter unless we turn them into crucifixes; and how can that be done except by seeing them as coming from the Lord? That we can do only if we are with Him. The Holy Hour may be a sacrifice, but the Lord does not make the week the unit of sacrifice. He tells us our cross is daily.

One moment in which Our Lord exulted was when He exclaimed in the midst of His disciples, "The hour has come" (John 17:1, Douay-Rheims). The word *hour* He used only in relation to His Passion and death. It was for that time, that hour, that the clock of time had been set in motion; it was for that hour that the world was created, the Lamb slain, the dust of earth prepared. To it, the patriarchs looked forward; to it, we look backward. Without it, there would be no Mass, no absolution, no pardon. Will the true priest shrink from such an hour, willing to be a priest but not a victim? To offer, but not to be offered? To be a grain of incense but unready to be consumed in the fire? Rather must he each day take up his cross of watching, saying with the Sacred Heart, "The hour has come."

Each day, while it is in his power to do so, because there will be a day and an hour that will not be his, over which he will have no control, for "that day and that hour you speak of, they are known to nobody, not even to the angels in heaven" (Mark 13:32).

It is not conceivable that a priest who has sanctified each day with its Hour will ever be rejected by the Judge. If Our Lord puts the day and the hour together to make it a symbol of judgment, then shall not we put the day and the hour together unto salvation, unto joy, and unto love? "Blessed is that servant who is found doing this when his Lord comes" (Luke 12:43).

It may be objected that an hour a day taken out of priestly work means that much less good can be done. The very same objection was made to Paul's imprisonment. Yet, from his prison, St. Paul wrote to the Philippians to reassure them that, even if not actively preaching, he was doing good. Each priest in prayer can say, like Paul in prison:

I hasten to assure you, brethren, that my circumstances here have only had the effect of spreading the gospel further; so widely has my imprisonment become known, in Christ's honor, throughout the praetorium and to all the world beyond. (Phil. 1:12–13)

All the things that were happening to him there were furthering the Gospel. We all stand committed to Christ under a spiritual obligation to maintain a clear and decisive loyalty, not only for our own sakes but also for the sakes of all whom our steadfastness and watchfulness will strengthen. The daily Holy Hour is a limitation on time, but a limitation that is conquered by a superior spiritual good. By human standards, nothing could be a greater waste than Paul in prison, just when Christianity was beginning to conquer the world. The same might be said of a pastor beginning a parish. Nothing could seem more wasteful than to sacrifice an hour for the Lord. But God's ways are different. The apparent reverse and discomfiture of man is turned into the triumph of truth. Mercies are garnered, and resources found hidden by the priest who knocks on the tabernacle door.

Every pastor may properly ask if he should not give more attention to the tabernacle and the altar in his church, in order to emphasize the Real Presence. An altar, which looks like a table, and a tabernacle, which looks like a box, help little to bring home to the viewer the Divine Presence. Would not the tabernacle perhaps be enriched by restoring the two cherubs prescribed under the Law of Moses?

The pastor's primary concern should be the tabernacle, not the rectory, not the ego, but the Lord; not his comfort, but God's glory. Wall-to-wall carpeting in a rectory goes poorly with an altar and tabernacle that look like a house on stilts. Should not the King have a better home than his representative? First things first, as David sang:

> Never will I come beneath the roof of my house, or climb up into the bed that is strewn for me; never shall these eyes have sleep, these eyelids close until I have found the Lord a home, the great God of Jacob a dwelling place.... Let thy priests go clad in the vesture of innocence; thy faithful people cry aloud with rejoicing. (Ps. 131:3–5, 9 [132:4–5, 9])

Some can be forgetful of the Eucharist, as Saul was unmindful of the ark. But David contrasted his own comfortable home with the poverty of the ark: "Here am I dwelling in a house all of cedar, while God's ark has nothing better than curtains of hide about it!" (2 Kings [2 Sam.] 7:2).

David could not allow the eternal God to dwell in an unfitting abode. The Lord rebukes those who build fine houses while neglecting His Temple:

> Listen, the Lord said [to them through the prophet Haggai], is it not too early yet for you to have roofs over your heads, and my temple in ruins?... To your own houses you run helter-skelter, and my temple in ruins! That is why the skies are forbidden to rain on you. (Haggai 1:3–4, 9–10)

But while we build churches worthy of the Eucharistic Lord, we will give 10 percent of the cost to build humble homes for the same Lord in Africa and Asia. He who makes the daily Hour will think of this, for he knows that his parish must be a victimhood, as it is also a royal priesthood.

There will come moments when the Hour is difficult—most often on vacation, but sometimes in great distress. What, then, gives the priest courage? This may be a time of darkness, as when the Greeks had come to Our Lord saying, "We wish to see Jesus," probably because of the majesty and beauty of appearance that they revered so highly as followers of Apollo (John 12:21). But He pointed to His torn and battered Self on a hill and added that only through the Cross in their lives will there ever be beauty of soul in the newness of life.

He then paused for a moment as His soul was seized by a frightening apprehension of the Passion and being "made sin," of being betrayed, crucified, and abandoned. Out from the depths of His Sacred Heart welled these words: "And now my soul is distressed. What am I to say? I will say, Father, save me from undergoing this hour of trial; And yet I have only reached this hour of trial that I might undergo it" (John 12:27).

These are almost the same words that He used later on in the Garden of Gethsemane—words that are inexplicable except for the fact that He was bearing the burden of the world's sins. It was only natural for Our Blessed Lord to undergo a struggle inasmuch as He was a perfect man. But it was not the physical sufferings, alone that troubled Him; He, like Stoics, philosophers, men, and women of all ages, could have been calm in the face of great physical trials. But His distress was directed less to the pain, and more to the consciousness of the sins of the world, which demanded these sufferings. The more He loved those for whom He was the ransom, the more His anguish would increase, as it is the faults of friends rather than enemies, which most disturb hearts!

He certainly was not asking to be saved from the Cross, since He reprimanded His Apostles for trying to dissuade Him. Two opposites were united in Him, separated only in utterance: the desire for release and submission to the Father's will. By laying bare His own soul, He told the Greeks that self-sacrifice was not easy. They were not to be fanatics about wanting to die, for nature does not want to crucify itself; but on the other hand, they were not to turn their eyes from the Cross in cowardly dread. In His own case, now as always, the most sorrowful moods pass into the most blissful; there is never the Cross without the Resurrection; the "Hour" in which evil has mastery passes quickly into the "Day" in which God is Victor.

And as, at that moment, there came to Him a Voice from heaven, so there will come to the priest-victim a voice from the tabernacle.

The Incarnation of Our Lord and Savior, Jesus Christ

Love is naturally expansive, but Divine Love is creative. Love told the secret of its goodness to nothingness, and that was creation. Love made something like unto its own image and likeness, and that was man. Love is prodigal of its gifts, and that was the elevation of man to the adoptive sonship of God. Love must always run risks of not being loved in return, for love is free. The human heart refused to return that love in the only way in which love can ever be shown—namely, by confidence and trust in a moment of trial. Man thus lost the gifts of God, darkened his intellect, weakened his will, and brought the first or original sin into the world, for sin is ultimately a refusal to love.

It was the refusal of man to love the best that created the most difficult problem in the whole history of humanity—namely, the problem of restoring man to the favor of Divine Love. In short, the problem was this: man had sinned, but his sin was not merely a rebellion against another man, but a revolt against the Infinite Love of God. Therefore, his sin was infinite.

Such is one side of the problem. The other side is this: every infraction or violation of a law demands reparation or atonement. Since God is Infinite Love, He might pardon man and forget the injury, but pardon without compensation would eclipse the justice, which is the nature of God. Without setting any limits to the mercy of God, one could understand His action better if His mercy was preceded by a satisfaction for sin, for one can never be merciful unless he is just. Mercy is the overflow of justice.

But assuming that man should give satisfaction, could he satisfy adequately for his sin? No, because the satisfaction or reparation or atonement that man had to offer was only finite.

Man, who is finite, owes an infinite debt. But how can a man who owes a million pay the debt with a cent? How can the human atone to the divine? How can justice and mercy be reconciled? If satisfaction is ever to be made for the Fall of man, the finite and the infinite, the human and the divine, God and man must in some way be linked together. It would not do for God alone to come down and suffer as God alone; for then, He would not have anything in common with man; the sin was not God's but man's. It would not do for man alone to suffer or atone, for the merit of his sufferings would be only finite. If the satisfaction were to be complete, two conditions would have to be fulfilled: man would have to be man to act as man and to atone; and man would have to be God in order that his sufferings would have an infinite value. But in order that the finite and the infinite should not be acting as two distinct personalities, and in order that infinite merit should result from man's suffering, God and man in some way would have to become one, or in other words, there would have to be a God-man. If justice and mercy were to be reconciled, there would have to be an Incarnation, which means God's assuming a human nature in such a way that He would be true God and true man. There would have to be a union of God and man, and this union took place in the birth of Our Lord and Savior, Jesus Christ.

Love tends to become like the one loved; in fact, it even wishes to become one with the one loved. God loved unworthy man. He willed to become one with him, and that was the Incarnation. One night, there went out over the stillness of an evening breeze, out over the white chalk hills of Bethlehem, a cry, a gentle cry. The sea did not hear the cry, for the sea was filled with its own voice. The earth did not hear the cry, for the earth slept. The great men of the earth did not hear the cry, for they could not understand how a child could be greater than a man. The kings of the earth did not hear the cry, for they could not fathom how a king could be born in a stable. There were only two classes of men who heard the cry that night: shepherds and Wise Men. Shepherds: those who know they know nothing. Wise Men: those who know they do not know everything. Shepherds: poor, simple men who knew only how to tend their flocks; who perhaps could not tell who the governor of Judea was; who, perhaps, did not know a single line of Virgil, though there was not a Roman who could not quote from him. On the other hand, there were the Wise Men; not kings, but teachers of kings; men who knew how to read the stars, to tell the story of their movements; men who were constantly bent on discovery. Both of these heard the cry. The Shepherds found their Shepherd; the Wise Men discovered Wisdom. And the Shepherd and the Wisdom was a Babe in a crib.

He who is born without a mother in heaven is born without a father on earth. He who made His mother is born of His mother. He who made all flesh is born of flesh. "The bird that built the nest is hatched therein."[11] Maker of the sun, under the sun; Molder of the earth, on the earth; Ineffably Wise, a little infant; filling the world, lying in a manger; ruling the stars, suckling a breast; the mirth of heaven weeps, God becomes man; Creator, a creature. Rich becomes poor; Divinity, incarnate; Majesty, subjugated; Liberty, captive; Eternity, time; Master, a servant; Truth, accused; Judge, judged; Justice, condemned; Lord, scourged; Power, bound with ropes; King, crowned with thorns; Salvation, wounded; Life, dead. "The Eternal Word is dumb." Marvel of marvels! Union of unions! Three mysterious unions in one: divinity and humanity; virginity and fecundity; faith and the heart of man.

It takes a divine, an infinite Being to use the very instruments of defeat as the instruments of victory. The Fall came through three realities: first, a disobedient man, Adam; second, a proud woman, Eve; third, a tree. The reconciliation and redemption of man came through these same

---

[11] Robert Southwell, "The Nativity of Christ," line 2.

three. For the disobedient man, Adam, was the obedient new Adam of the human race, Christ; for the proud Eve, there was the humble Mary; and for the tree, the Cross.

Our Lord did not walk about the earth forever, telling people platitudes about truth. He was not just explaining truth, defeat, resignation, and sacrifice. Everyone else did this. The goal He was seeking was death. From the beginning to the end, only one vision was before His eyes: He was going to die—not die because He could not help it, but die because He willed it. Death was not an incident in His career; it was not an accident in His plan—it was the one business He had to do.

All during His redeeming life, He looked forward to His redemptive death. He anticipated His blood-shedding on Calvary by His circumcision at eight days of age. At the beginning of His public ministry, His presence inspired John to cry out to his disciples at the Jordan: "Behold the Lamb of God" (John 1:29). He answered to the confession of His divinity by Peter at Caesarea Philippi that He "must suffer many things from the elders and scribes and chief priests, and be put to death, and on the third day rise again" (Matt. 16:21, Douay-Rheims); the leaden-weighted days caused Him to cry out in beautiful impatience: "I have a baptism to be baptized with; and how distressed I am until it is accomplished!" (see Luke 12:50).

To the member of the Sanhedrin who would seek a sign, He foretold His death on the Cross. He answered: "As Moses lifted up the serpent in the desert, so must the Son of man be lifted up: that whosoever believeth in him, may not perish; but may have life everlasting" (John 3:14–15, Douay-Rheims). To the Pharisees, who were as sheep without a shepherd, He spoke: "I am the good shepherd. The good shepherd lays down his life for his sheep ... and I lay down my life for my sheep.... No one takes it from me, but I lay it down of myself. I have power to lay it down, and I have power to take it up again. Such is the command I have received from my Father" (see John 10:11, 15, 18). To all men of all times who would forget that He is come as our Redeemer and Savior, He speaks the most tender words that were ever caught up on this sinful earth: "For God so loved the world that he gave his only-begotten Son, that those who believe in him may not perish, but may have life everlasting. For God did not send his Son into the world in order to judge the world, but that the world might be saved through him" (see John 3:16–17).

Prayer of St. Augustine

Lord Jesus, may I know myself and know Thee and desire nothing save only Thee. May I hate myself and love Thee. May I do everything for the sake of Thee. May I humble myself and exalt Thee. May I think of nothing except Thee. May I die to myself and live in Thee. May I receive whatever happens as from Thee. May I banish self and follow Thee and ever desire to follow Thee. May I fly from myself and fly to Thee, that I may deserve to be defended by Thee. May I fear for myself and fear Thee and be among those who are chosen by Thee. May I distrust myself and trust in Thee. May I be willing to obey on account of Thee. May I cling to nothing but to Thee. May I be poor for the sake of Thee. Look upon me that I may love Thee. Call me that I may see Thee, and ever and ever enjoy Thee. Amen. (*Raccolta*)

The Repentance and Confession of David after His Sin

Have mercy on me, O God, according to Thy great mercy. And according to the multitude of Thy tender mercies blot out my iniquity. Wash me yet more from my iniquity and cleanse me from my sin. For I know my iniquity, and my sin is always before me. To Thee only have I sinned, and have done evil before Thee: that Thou mayst be justified in Thy words, and mayst overcome when Thou art judged. For behold, I was conceived in iniquities, and in sins did my mother conceive me. For behold, Thou hast loved truth: the uncertain and hidden things of Thy wisdom Thou hast made manifest to me. Thou shalt sprinkle me with hyssop, and I shall be cleansed: Thou shalt wash me, and I shall be made whiter than snow. To my hearing Thou shalt give joy and gladness: and the bones that have been humbled shall rejoice. Turn away thy face from my sins, and blot out all my iniquities. Create a clean heart in me, O God: and renew a right spirit within my bowels. Cast me not away from Thy face, and take not Thy holy spirit from me. Restore unto me the joy of Thy salvation, and strengthen me with a perfect spirit. I will teach the unjust thy ways: and the wicked shall be converted to Thee. Deliver me from blood, O God, Thou God of my salvation: and my tongue shall extol thy justice. O Lord, Thou wilt open my lips: and my mouth shall declare Thy praise. For if Thou hadst desired sacrifice, I would indeed have given it: with burnt offerings, Thou wilt not be delighted. A sacrifice to God is an afflicted spirit: a contrite and humbled heart, O God, Thou wilt not despise. Deal favorably, O Lord, in Thy good will with Sion; that the walls of Jerusalem may be built up. Then shalt Thou accept the sacrifice of justice, oblations, and whole burnt offerings: then shall they lay calves upon Thy altar. (Ps. 50:3–21)

How Christ Lives in Us Today

How often we hear souls bemoan that they are so distant from Galilee and so removed from Jesus. The world is full of men and women who think of Our Lord solely and uniquely in terms of what their eyes can see, their ears can hear, and their hands can touch. How many there are who, starting with the truth that He was a great Teacher of commanding influence who walked the earth two thousand years ago, gather up the details of the scenery of the lake and hill country of Galilee, and use their imagination better to portray the exact circumstances of His earthly life; but here the appreciation of His life ends. They have learned habitually to think of Him as someone who belongs to human history, like Caesar, Washington, or Mohammed; they think of Him as one who lived on earth and passed away. But where He is, what His nature is, whether He can act upon us now, whether He can hear us, be approached by us, are thoughts that are contemptuously dismissed as belonging to the category of theological abstractions and foolish dogmas. These very souls may follow His example in such and such an instance, apply His Beatitudes to this or that circumstance of their life, look upon His life as a great sacrifice and inspiration; but beyond that, Christ means nothing to them. He is the greatest man who ever lived, but He is nothing more. They indeed are among those of whom St. Paul said that they know Christ only according to the flesh.

It must be admitted that the continued sensible and visible presence of our Savior would have been a continuous inspiration to our lives, but we must not forget that He Himself said the night before He died: "It is expedient for you that I depart" (John 16:7). Strange words, these. Why should they be spoken at a moment when He had weaned the hearts of His Apostles away from their nets, boats, and custom tables, and had entwined them so closely about His own Sacred Heart? How could it be expedient for them that He go? It was expedient for Him to go in order that He might be nearer to us. This is the very reason He gave for His going: "For if I do not go, the Advocate will not come to you; but if I go, I will send him to you.... A little while and you shall see me no longer; and again a little while, and you shall see me because I go to the Father ... I will see you again, and your heart shall rejoice; and your joy no one shall take from you" (see John 16:7–8, 16, 22).

In these solemn words spoken on the eve of His Crucifixion, He explicitly stated that He was going back to the boundless depths of His Father's Life whence He came, but His going would not leave them orphans, for He would come again in a new way—namely, by His Spirit. Our Lord was equivalently saying that if He remained on earth in His physical life, He would have been only an example to be copied; but if He went to His Father and sent His Spirit, then He would be a life to be lived. If he remained on earth, He would always have been outside us, external to us; an external voice, an external life, an eternal example—He could never be possessed other than by an embrace.

But once He ascended into heaven and sat at the right hand of the Father in the glory that is His, then He could send His Spirit into our souls, so that He would be with us not as an external Person, but as a living Soul. Then He would be not just a mere something mechanical to be copied, but a something vital to be reproduced; not a something external to be portrayed in our lives, but a something living to be developed within us. His Ascension into Heaven, and His sending of His Spirit alone make it possible for Him to unite Himself wholly with us, to take up His abode with us, Body and Blood, Soul and Divinity, and to be in the strictest sense of the term "Christ in us." It was expedient, therefore, that He go. Otherwise, He would have belonged to history and to a country. Now He belongs to men.

Thanks to His Invisible Spirit, which He sends into His Mystical Body, Christ is living now on earth just as really and truly as He was living in Galilee twenty centuries ago. In a certain sense He is closer to us now than then, for His very body then made Him external to us, but thanks to His Spirit, He can now live in us as the very Soul of our soul, the very Spirit of our spirit, the Truth of our mind, the Love of our heart, and the Desire of our will. Thus, the life of Christ is transferred by the Spirit from the region of purely historical studies, which we investigate with our reason, to the realm of spiritual experience, where He speaks directly to our souls. It may have been a great consolation for the Canaanite woman to have touched the hem of His garment, for Magdalene to have kissed His feet, for John to have leaned on His breast the night of the Last Supper, but all these intimacies are external. They have great force and appeal because they are sensible, but none of them can even vaguely approximate the union, the intimacy, that comes of possessing Christ inwardly, thanks to His Holy Spirit. The greatest joys of life are those that come from unity. We never reach the height of unity until there is a fusion of loves, of thoughts, and of desires, a unity so profound that we think with the one we love, love with the one we love, desire what he desires; and this unity is found in its perfection when the soul is made one with the Spirit of Christ, which is the Spirit of God. The joys that come from human friendships, even the noblest, are but the shadows and fond reflections of the joy of a soul possessed of the Spirit of Christ. Elevate human happiness, which comes from union with the one loved, to the extremest point the heart can endure, and even that is but a spark compared with the Great Flame of the Spirit of Christ burning in a soul that loves Him.

What precisely is this life of Christ in the baptized soul? It is grace, a supernatural gift bestowed on us through the merits of Jesus Christ for our salvation.

The whole order of creation affords us an analogy of the gift quality of grace. If a stone—say, the rock of Gibraltar—should suddenly break out into bloom, it would be something transcending its nature. If a rose one day would become conscious, and see and feel and touch, it would be a supranatural act—an act totally undue to the nature of the rose as such. If an animal would break out into a reasoning process and speak words of wisdom, it would be a supranatural act, for it is not in the nature of an animal to be rational. So too, but in a far more rigorous manner, if man, who by nature is a creature of God, becomes a child of God, a member of the family of the Trinity, and a brother of Jesus Christ, it is a supernatural act for man, and a gift that surpasses all the exigencies and powers of his nature, even more than blooming surpasses the nature and powers of marble.

Grace makes man a "new creature," infinitely higher than his former condition, more than an animal would be if it spoke with the wisdom of Socrates. There is nothing in all creation like that gift by which God calls man a son, and man calls God "Father." The difference between mere human life and human life rendered deiform by grace is not one of development but of generation. The source of life in both cases is as different as human and divine paternity. The distance, that separates some minerals from the vegetable kingdom, may be only a hair's breadth—but the distance that separates human life and divine life is infinite. "No one can pass from thence hence" (see Luke 16:26).

The world, in the eyes of God, is divided into two classes, the sons of men and the sons of God. All are called to be sons of God, but not all accept the gift worthily, believing that if they should take Christ as their portion, they would have naught else besides. It is to forget that the whole contains the parts and that in perfect life, we have the joys of finite life in an infinite degree. Both types of sons are born, the one according to the flesh, the other according to the spirit. "That which is born of the flesh is flesh; and that which is born of the Spirit is spirit" (John 3:6). Being born of the flesh incorporates us into the life of Adam; being born of the spirit—of the waters of the Holy Spirit—incorporates us into the life of Christ. The sons of God are twice born; the sons of men once born. There is more difference between two souls on this earth, one in the state of grace and the other not in that state, than there is between two souls, one in the state of grace in this life and the other enjoying the eternal blessedness of Heaven. The reason is that grace is the germ of glory and someday will blossom into glory, just as the acorn someday will become the oak. But the soul not possessed with grace has no such potencies in it. "Beloved," says St. John, "now we are the children of God, and it has not yet appeared what we shall be. We know that, when he appears, we shall be like to him, for we shall see him just as he is" (1 John 3:2).

The Different Effects of Nature and Grace
(Thomas à Kempis, *The Imitation of Christ*, book 3, chapter 54)

Son, observe diligently the motions of *nature* and *grace*; for they move very opposite ways, and very subtly, and can hardly be distinguished but by a spiritual man, and one who is internally illuminated.

All men, indeed, aim at good, and pretend to something of good in what they do and say: therefore, under the appearance of good, many are deceived.

Nature is crafty, and draws away many; ensnares them, and deceives them, and always intends herself for her end. But *grace* walks with simplicity, turns away from all appearance of evil, offers no deceits, and does all things purely for God, in whom also she rests as in her last end.

Nature is unwilling to be mortified, or to be restrained, or to be overcome, or to be subject; neither will she of her own accord be brought under. But *grace* studies the mortification of her own self, resists sensuality, seeks to be subject, covets to be overcome, aims not at following her own liberty, loves to be kept under discipline, and desires not to have the command over anyone; but under God ever to live, stand, and be; and for God's sake is ever ready humbly to bow down herself under all human creatures.

Nature labors for her own interest, and thinks what gain she may reap from others. But *grace* considers not what may be advantageous and profitable to herself but rather what may be profitable to many.

Nature willingly receives honor and respect. But *grace* faithfully attributes all honor and glory to God.

Nature is afraid of being put to shame and despised. But *grace* is glad to suffer reproach for the name of Jesus.

Nature loves idleness and bodily rest. But *grace* cannot be idle and willingly embraces labor.

Nature seeks to have things that are curious and fine, and does not care for things that are cheap and coarse. But *grace* is pleased with that which is plain and humble, rejects not coarse things, nor refuses to be clad in old clothes.

Nature has regard to temporal things, rejoices at earthly gain, is troubled at losses, and is provoked at every slight, injurious word. But *grace* attends to things eternal, and cleaves not to those that pass with time; neither is she disturbed at the loss of things, nor exasperated with hard words, for she places her treasure and her joy in heaven, where nothing is lost.

Nature is covetous, and is more willing to take than to give, and loves to have things to herself. But *grace* is bountiful and openhearted, avoids selfishness, is contented with little, and judges it more happy to give than to receive.

Nature inclines to creatures, to her own flesh, to vanities, and to gadding abroad. But *grace* draws to God and to virtue, renounces creatures, flies the world, hates the desires of the flesh, restrains wandering about, and is ashamed to appear in public.

Nature willingly receives exterior comfort, in which she may be sensibly delighted. But *grace* seeks to be comforted in God alone, and beyond all things visible, to be delighted in the Sovereign Good.

Nature does all for her own lucre and interest; she can do nothing gratis, but hopes to gain something equal or better, or praise, or favor for her good deeds, and covets to have her actions and gifts much valued.

But *grace* seeks nothing temporal, nor requires any other recompense but God alone for her reward, nor desires anything more of the necessaries of this life that may be serviceable for the obtaining a happy eternity.

Nature rejoices in a multitude of friends and kindred; she glories in the nobility of her stock and descent; she fawns on them that are in power, flatters the rich, and applauds such as are like herself. But *grace* loves even her enemies, and is not puffed up with having a great many friends, nor has any value for family or birth, unless when joined to greater virtue; she rather favors the poor than the rich; she has more compassion for the innocent than the powerful; she rejoices with him that loves the truth, and not with the deceitful; she ever exhorts the good to be zealous for better gifts, and to become like to the Son of God by the exercise of virtues.

Nature easily complains of want and of trouble. But *grace* bears poverty with constancy.

Nature turns all things to herself, and for herself, she labors and disputes. But *grace* refers all things to God, from whom all originally proceed; she attributes no good to herself, nor does she arrogantly presume of herself: she does not contend, nor prefer her own opinion to others, but in every sense and understanding she submits herself to the eternal wisdom and the divine examination.

Nature covets to know secrets, and to hear news; is willing to appear abroad, and to have experience of many things by the senses; desires to be taken notice of and to do such things as may procure praise and admiration. But *grace* cares not for the hearing of news and curious things, because all this springs from the old corruption since nothing is new or lasting upon earth.

Grace teaches, therefore, to restrain the senses, to avoid vain complacency and ostentation, humbly to hide those things that are worthy of praise and admiration, and from everything, and in every knowledge, to seek the fruit of spiritual profit, and the praise and honor of God.

She desires not to have herself for what belongs to her extolled but wishes that God may be blessed in his gifts, who bestows all through mere love.

This *grace* is a supernatural light, and a certain special gift of God, and the proper mark of the elect, and the pledge of eternal salvation, which elevates a man from things of the earth to the love of heavenly things, and, if carnal, makes him spiritual.

Wherefore, by how much the more nature is kept down and subdued, with so much the greater abundance *grace* is infused, and the inward man, by new visitations, is daily more reformed according to the image of God.

How That Divine Life Is Lost and Our Final End

Sin is the killing of the Christ life in our souls. Our conscience is the courtroom of Pilate. Daily and hourly, Barabbas and Christ are brought before us. Barabbas comes as vice, murder, blasphemy—Christ comes as virtue, love, and purity. Which of the two shall be released?

If we die in the state of sin, we shall be judged as sinners. What is judgment? Judgment may be considered both from God's point of view and from our point of view.

From God's point of view, judgment is a recognition. Two souls appear before the sight of God in that split-second after death. One is in the state of grace; the other is not. The Judge looks into the soul in the state of grace. He sees there a resemblance to His nature, for grace is a participation in divine nature. Just as a mother knows her child because of the resemblance of nature, so too, God knows His own children by resemblance of nature. If they are born of Him, He knows it. Seeing in that soul His likeness, the Sovereign Judge, Our Lord and Savior Jesus Christ says in effect: "Come, ye blessed of my Father. I have taught you to pray, 'Our Father.' I am the natural Son; you, the adopted son. Come into the kingdom I have prepared for you from all eternity."

The other soul, not possessing the family traits and likeness of the Trinity, meets an entirely different reception from the Judge. As a mother knows that her neighbor's son is not her own, because there is no participation in nature, so, too, Jesus Christ, seeing in the sinful soul no participation of His nature, can only say those words that signify nonrecognition: "I know you not" (see Matt. 7:23); and it is a terrible thing not to be known by God!

Such is judgment from the divine point of view. From the human point of view, it is also a recognition, but a recognition of unfitness or fitness. A very distinguished visitor is announced at the door, but I am in my working clothes, and my hands and face are dirty. I am in no condition to present myself before such an august personage, and I refuse to see him until I can improve my appearance. A soul stained with sin acts very much the same when it goes before the judgment seat of God. It sees, on one hand, His majesty, His purity, His brilliance, and, on the other, its own baseness, its sinfulness, and its unworthiness. It does not entreat or argue; it does not plead a case — it sees; and from out of the depths comes its own judgment, "Oh, Lord, I am not worthy." The soul that is stained with venial sins casts itself into purgatory to wash its baptismal robes, but the soul irremediably stained — the soul dead to divine life — casts itself into hell just as naturally as a stone that is released from my hand falls to the ground.

But is there a hell? The modern world no longer believes in it. True it is that many of our present-day prophets deny hell, and that makes us ask the reason for the denial. The reason is probably psychological.

There are two possible orientations for a man. Either he must adapt his life to dogmas, or he must adapt dogmas to his life. If we do not live as we think, we soon begin to think as we live. If our life is not regulated in accordance with the Gospel, then the thought of hell is a very uncomfortable kind of thought. To ease my conscience, I must deny it. I must suit a dogma to my mode of life. And this is borne out by experience. Some believe in hell, fear it, hate it, and avoid sin. Others love sin, deny hell, but always fear it.

But granted that such be the reason for its denial, these same prophets will ask, "How do you know there is a hell?" Very clearly, because Jesus Christ said there is. Either there is a hell, or Infinite Truth is a liar. I cannot accept the second proposition, so I must accept the first.

Heaven and hell are not mere afterthoughts in the divine plan. God did not, by a second act of His will and omnipotence, create heaven and hell to reward and punish those who obey or disobey His divine law. They are not arbitrary decrees—mere things to patch up an original plan disturbed by sin. No law can exist without sanction. If there were no hell in the present order of salvation, what would be the consequence? It would mean that whatever evil we did, and regardless of how long we did it and the hatred with which we did it, God would all the while be indifferent to our moral acts; and this would be another way of saying that law is indifferent to lawlessness.

All our misconceptions concerning heaven and hell are founded on our inability to see how they are bound up necessarily with our acts in the moral order. There are many who regard heaven only as an arbitrary reward for a good life, a kind of token in appreciation of our victory, as a silver loving cup is awarded to the winner of a race. Such is not the whole truth. Heaven is not related to a good Christian life in the same way a silver cup is related to the winning of a race, for the silver cup may or may not follow the victory; it is not something inseparably bound up with it—something else might be given or perhaps nothing at all. Rather, heaven is related to a Christian life as learning is related to study; that is why theologians call grace the "seed of glory." If I study, I acquire knowledge by that very act; the two are inseparable, one being the fruition of the other. And in this connection, it is well to remember that heaven, in the present constitution of God's world, is not merely a reward; it is, in a certain sense, a "right," the right of heirs—for we are heirs of the kingdom of heaven in virtue of the gift of divine adoption into the sonship of God by a heavenly Father.

Hell, too, is often explained too exclusively in terms of arbitrariness. It is made to appear as a kind of punishment wholly unrelated to a life of sin and the abandonment of the gift of God. Hell is not related to an evil life as a spanking is related to an act of disobedience, for such a punishment need not necessarily follow the act. Rather, hell is bound up with an evil life in precisely the same way as blindness is related to the plucking out of an eye. If I lose my eye, I am blind necessarily, and if I rebel against God, refuse His pardon, and die in sin, I must suffer hell as a consequence. There is equity in human law, and there is equity in the divine law. A sin involves, first, a turning away from God; second, a turning to creatures. Because of the first element, the sinner suffers the pain of loss or the deprivation of the Beatific Vision. Because of the turning to creatures, the sinner suffers the pain of sense, which is a punishment by created things for the abuse of created things, and this is commonly referred to as "hellfire."

The difference between the pain of loss and the pain of sense is that the former is caused by the absence of something and the latter by the presence of something. Of the two pains, the first is the more terrible, for it is the final and never-ceasing frustration of the craving of an immortal being; it is the missing of the goal of life; it is the having failed so utterly as never to admit of another start; it is to want God and yet hate oneself for wanting Him; it is an asking never to receive, a seeking never to find, a knocking at a gate eternally closed; it is, above all, a void created by the absence of the life, the truth, and the love that the soul eternally craves. How eagerly souls yearn for life; how tenaciously they cling to even a straw to save from drowning! How they desire to prolong life even into eternity! What must it be then to miss, not a long human life, but the very life of all living! It is a kind of living death, like waking up in a sepulcher.

Truth, too, is the desire of souls. Knowledge is a passion, and the human deprival of it is pain, as is so forcibly brought home to us when we are deprived of the knowledge of a secret in which others share. What must it be, then, to be deprived not of an earthly truth, not something that we could learn later on perhaps, but the truth outside of which there is no truth or knowledge or wisdom at all? It would be worse than earthly life without sun or moon, a kind of cavernous darkness in which one moves about knowing that one might have known the light of truth but would not.

Finally, how dull an earthly life would be without the affection or the love of parents, brothers, sisters, and friends! How heavy our hearts would be if every other heart turned to stone! Then what must it be to be deprived of the love without which there is no love? It is to have one's heart stolen and still be able to live without it.

Heaven and hell are the natural and inseparable results of acts, good and bad, in the supernatural order. This life is the springtime; judgment is the harvest. "For what things a man shall sow, those also shall he reap. For he that soweth in his flesh, of the flesh also shall reap corruption. But he that soweth in the spirit shall reap life everlasting" (Gal. 6:8).

Why do souls go to hell? In the last analysis, souls go to hell for one great reason: they refuse to love. Love pardons everything except one thing—refusal to love. A young man loves a maiden. He makes known his affection toward her, showers her with gifts, bestows on her more than the ordinary share of the courtesies of life, but his love is repulsed. Keeping it pure, he pursues, but all in vain; she turns a deaf ear to his wooing. Love, so long denied and cast aside, suddenly reaches a point where it will cry out: "All right, love can do no more, I am through now; we are finished." It has reached the point of abandonment.

God is the Divine Lover. As the Hound of Heaven, He is continually in pursuit of souls. Way back in the agelessness of eternity, He loved us with an eternal love. When time begins for an individual soul, He gives it the riches of nature, calls it to be an adopted son, feeds it on His own substance, and makes it an heir of Heaven. But that soul may soon forget such goodness, and yet God does not forget to love. He pursues the soul, sends discontent deep into it to bring it back to Him, cuts purposely across its path to manifest His presence, sends His ambassadors to it, lavishes it with medicinal graces; and still, Divine Love is spurned. Finally, rejected more often than seventy times seven, Divine Love abandons the pursuit of such a soul that turns from Him at the end of its lease on life and cries out: "It is finished. Love can do no more." And it is a terrible thing not to be loved, and most of all not to be loved by Love. That is hell. Hell is a place where there is no love.

On Considering One's Death

(Thomas à Kempis, *The Imitation of Christ*, book 1, chapter 23)

Very quickly, your life here will end; consider then, what may be in store for you elsewhere.

A man is here today, and tomorrow he is vanished. And when he is taken away from sight, he is quickly also out of mind.

Oh! the dullness and hardness of man's heart, which only thinks on what is present, and looks not forward to things to come.

Therefore, in every deed and every thought, act as though you were to die this very day. If you had a good conscience, you would not fear death very much.

It were better for you to avoid sin than to be afraid of death.

If you are not prepared today, how will you be prepared tomorrow?

Tomorrow is an uncertain day; and how do you know you will be alive tomorrow?

What benefit is it to live long, when we advance so little?

Ah! long life does not always make us better but often adds to our guilt.

Would to God we had behaved ourselves well in this world, even for one day!

Many count the years of their conversion, but oftentimes the fruit of amendment is small. If it be frightful to die, perhaps it will be more dangerous to live longer.

Blessed is he that has always the hour of his death before his eyes, and every day disposes himself to die.

If you have ever seen a man die, remember that you too must also pass the same way. In the morning, imagine that you may not live until night; and when evening comes, presume not to promise yourself the next morning.

Be always ready and live in such manner that death may never find you unprovided. Many die suddenly, and when they little think of it: *For the Son of Man will come at the hour when he is not looked for* (Matt. 24:44). When that last hour shall come, then you will begin to have quite other thoughts of your whole past life; and you will be exceedingly grieved that you have been so negligent and remiss.

How happy and prudent is he who strives to be such now in this life, as he desires to be found at his death. For it will give a man a great confidence of dying happily if he has a perfect contempt of the world, a fervent desire of advancing in virtue, a love for discipline, the spirit of penance, a ready obedience, self-denial, and patience in bearing all adversities for the love of Christ.

You can do many good things when in good health; but when you are sick, I know not what you will be able to do.

Few are improved by sickness; they also that travel much abroad seldom become holy.

Trust not in your friends and relatives, and do not put off the care of your soul till later; for who will care when you are gone?

It is better now to provide in time and send some good ahead of you than to trust others helping you after your death.

If you do not care for your own welfare now, who will care when you are gone?

The present time is very precious. *Behold now is the acceptable time; behold, now is the day of salvation* (2 Cor. 6:2).

But it is greatly to be lamented, that you do not spend this time more profitably, where you might purchase everlasting life in a better way! The time will come when you will wish for one day or hour to amend, and I know not whether you will obtain it.

O my dearly beloved, from how great a danger you can free yourself; from how great a fear may you be freed, if you will but now be always fearful and mindful of death!

Strive now so to live, that in the hour of your death you will rather rejoice than fear.

Learn now to despise all things, that you will then begin to live with Christ. Learn now to die to the world, that you may then freely go to Christ. Chastise your body now by penance, that you may then have an assured confidence.

Ah, fool! Why do you think to live long, when you are not sure of one day? How many, thinking to live long, have been deceived, and unexpectedly have been snatched away!

How often have you heard related that such a one was slain by sword; another drowned; another, falling from on high, broke his neck; this man died at the table; that other came to his end when he was at play? Some have perished by fire; some by the sword; some by pestilence; and some by robbers. Thus, death is the end of all, and man's life passes suddenly like a shadow.

Who will remember you when you are dead, and who will pray for you?

Do now, beloved, do now all you can, because you know not when you shall die, nor what fate will be after death.

Gather for yourself the riches of immortality while you have time; think of nothing but your salvation; care for nothing but the things of God.

Make friends for yourself now, by honoring the saints of God, by imitating their actions so that when you shall depart from this life, they may receive you into everlasting dwellings (see Luke 16:9).

Keep yourself as a pilgrim, and a stranger upon earth, to whom the affairs of this world do not in the least belong.

Keep your heart free, and raised upward to God, because you have not here a lasting home.

To Him direct your daily prayers, with sighs and tears; that after death, your spirit may be worthy to pass happily to Our Lord. Amen.

The Duty of Self-Denial

(St. John Henry Newman, *Parochial and Plain Sermons*, volume 7, sermon 7)

Self-denial of some kind or other is involved, as is evident, in the very notion of renewal and holy obedience. To change our hearts is to learn to love things that we do not naturally love — to unlearn the love of this world; but this involves, of course, a thwarting of our natural wishes and tastes. To be righteous and obedient implies self-command, but to possess power, we must have gained it; nor can we gain it without a vigorous struggle, a persevering warfare against ourselves. The very notion of being religious implies self-denial, because, by nature, we do not love religion....

It is our duty not only to deny ourselves in what is sinful but even in a certain measure, in lawful things, to keep a restraint over ourselves even in innocent pleasures and enjoyments....

Fasting is clearly a Christian duty, as our Savior implies in His Sermon on the Mount. Now, what is fasting but refraining from what is lawful; not merely from what is sinful, but what is innocent — from that bread that we might lawfully take and eat with thanksgiving, but which at certain times we do not take, in order to deny ourselves? Such is Christian self-denial — not merely a mortification of what is sinful, but an abstinence even from God's blessings.

Again consider the following declaration of our Savior: He first tells us, "How narrow the gate and close the way that leads to life! And few, there are who find it" (Matt. 7:14). And again: "Strive to enter by the narrow gate; for many, I tell you, will seek to enter and will not be able" (Luke 13:24). Then he explains to us what this peculiar difficulty of a Christian's life consists in: "If anyone comes to me and does not hate his father and mother, and wife and children, and brothers and sisters, yes, and even his own life, he cannot be my disciple" (Luke 14:26). Now whatever is precisely meant by this (which I will not stop here to inquire), so far is evident, that Our Lord enjoins a certain refraining, not merely from sin, but from innocent comforts and enjoyments of this life, or a self-denial in things lawful.

Again, He says, "If anyone wishes to come after me, let him deny himself, and take up his cross daily, and follow me" (Luke 9:23). Here he shows us from His own example what Christian self-denial is. It is taking on us a cross after His pattern, not a mere refraining from sin, for He had no sin, but a giving up what we might lawfully use. This was the peculiar character in which Christ came on earth. It was this spontaneous and exuberant self-denial that brought Him here. He who was one with God, took upon Himself our nature and suffered death. And why? To save us whom He needed not save. Thus, He denied Himself and took up His Cross. This is the very aspect, in which God, as revealed in Scripture, is distinguished from that exhibition of His glory, which nature gives us: power, wisdom, love, mercy, long-suffering—these attributes, though far more fully and clearly displayed in Scripture than in nature, are still, in their degree, seen on the face of the visible creation; but self-denial, if it may be said, this incomprehensible attribute of divine providence, is disclosed to us only in Scripture. "For God so loved the world that He gave his only-begotten Son" (John 3:16). Here is self-denial. And the Son of God so loved you, that "being rich, he became poor for your sakes" (2 Cor. 8:9). Here is our Savior's self-denial. "He pleased not Himself."

Such is Christian self-denial, and it is incumbent upon us for many reasons. The Christian denies himself in things lawful because he is aware of his own weakness and liability to sin; he dares not walk on the edge of a precipice; instead of going to the extreme of what is allowable, he keeps at a distance from evil, that he may be safe. He abstains lest he should not be temperate; he fasts lest he should eat and drink with the drunken. As is evident, many things are in themselves right and unexceptionable that are inexpedient in the case of a weak and sinful creature. His case is like that of a sick person; many kinds of food, good for a man in health, are hurtful when he is ill—wine is poison to a man in a fierce fever. And just so, many acts, thoughts, and feelings that would have been allowable in Adam before his fall are prejudicial or dangerous in man fallen. For instance, anger is not sinful in itself. St. Paul implies this when he says, "Be angry and do not sin" (Eph. 4:26). And our Savior on one occasion is said to have been angry, and He was sinless. Almighty God, too, is angry with the wicked. Anger, then, is not in itself a sinful feeling; but in man, constituted as he is, it is so highly dangerous to indulge it, that self-denial here is a duty from mere prudence. It is almost impossible for a man to be angry only so far as he ought to be; he will exceed the right limit; his anger will degenerate into pride, sullenness, malice, cruelty, revenge, and hatred. It will inflame his diseased soul and poison it. Therefore, he must abstain from it, as if it were in itself a sin (though it is not), for it is practically such to him.

If we have good health and are in easy circumstances, let us beware of high-mindedness, self-sufficiency, self-conceit, arrogance; of delicacy of living, indulgences, luxuries, comforts. Nothing is so likely to corrupt our hearts, and to seduce us from God, as to surround ourselves with comforts—to have things our own way—to be the center of a sort of world of things animate or inanimate, that minister to us. For then, in turn, we shall depend on them; they will become necessary to us; their very service and adulation will lead us to trust ourselves to them, and to idolize them.

What examples are there in Scripture of soft, luxurious men! Was it Abraham before the Law, who wandered through his days, without a home? Or Moses, who gave the Law, and died in the wilderness? Or David under the Law, who "had no proud looks," and was "as a weaned child" (see Ps. 130:2)? Or the prophets in the latter days of the Law, who wandered in sheep skins and goat skins? Or the Baptist, when the Gospel was superseding it, who was clad in raiment of camel's hair and ate the food of the wilderness? Or the Apostles, who were "the offscouring of all things" (1 Cor. 4:13)? Or our blessed Savior, who "had not a place to lay His head" (Matt. 8:20)? Who are the soft, luxurious men in Scripture? There was the rich man, who "fared sumptuously every day," and then "lifted up his eyes in hell, being in torments" (Luke 16:19, 23). There was that other, whose "ground brought forth plentifully," and who said, "Soul, thou hast much goods laid up for many years" (Luke 12:16, 19); and his soul was required of him that night. There was Demas, who forsook St. Paul, "having loved this present world" (2 Tim. 4:9)! And, alas! There was that highly favored, that divinely inspired king, rich and wise Solomon, whom it availed nothing to have measured the earth and numbered its inhabitants, when in his old age he "loved many strange women," and worshipped their gods (1 Kings 11:1, 4).

You need not attempt to draw any precise line between what is sinful and what is only allowable: look up to Christ and deny yourself everything, whatever its character, that you think He would have you relinquish. You need not calculate and measure if you love much: you need not perplex yourself with points of curiosity if you have a heart to venture after Him. True, difficulties will sometimes arise, but they will seldom be. He bids you take up your cross; therefore, accept the daily opportunities of yielding to others when you need not yield, and of doing unpleasant services that you might avoid. He bids those who would be highest to live as the lowest: therefore, turn from ambitious thoughts, and (as far as you religiously may) make resolves against taking on your authority and rule. He bids you sell and give alms; therefore, hate to spend money on yourself. Shut your eyes to praise, when it grows loud; set your face like a flint, when the world ridicules, and smile at its threats. Learn to master your heart, when it would burst forth into vehemence, or prolong a barren sorrow, or dissolve into unseasonable tenderness. Curb your tongue, and turn away your eye, lest you fall into temptation. Avoid the dangerous air that relaxes you, and brace yourself upon the heights. Be up at prayer "a great while before day," and seek the true, your only Bridegroom, "by night on your bed." So shall self-denial become natural to you, and a change come over you, gently and imperceptibly; and, like Jacob, you will lie down in the waste, and you will soon see angels, and a way opened for you into heaven.

On Judgment and the Punishment of Sinners
(Thomas à Kempis, *The Imitation of Christ*, book 1, chapter 24)

In all things look to the end, and how you shall be able to stand before a severe judge, from whom nothing is hidden; who takes no bribes, nor receives excuses, but will judge that which is just.

O most wretched and foolish sinner, what answer will you make to God, who knows all your sins; you who sometimes are afraid of the looks of an angry man?

Why do you not provide for yourself against the day of judgment, when no man can be excused or defended by another, but everyone shall have enough to do to answer for himself?

At present, your labor is profitable, your tears are acceptable, your sighs will be heard, and your sorrow is satisfactory and may purge away your sins.

A patient man has a great and wholesome purgatory, who, receiving injuries, is more concerned at another person's sin than his own wrong; who willingly prays for his adversaries, and from his heart forgives offenses; who delays not to ask forgiveness of others; who is easier moved to compassion than to anger; who frequently uses violence toward himself, and labors to bring the flesh wholly under subjection to the spirit.

It is better now to purge away our sins and root out vices than to reserve them to be purged hereafter.

Truly, we deceive ourselves through the inordinate love we bear to our flesh.

What other things shall that fire feed on but your sins?

The more you spare yourself now, and follow the flesh, the more grievously shall you suffer hereafter, and the more fuel you will lay up for that fire.

In what things a man has more sinned, in those shall he be more heavily punished.

There, the slothful will be pricked forward with burning goads, and the glutton will be tormented with extreme hunger and thirst.

There the luxurious and the lovers of pleasure will be covered all over with burning pitch and stinking brimstone; and the envious, like mad dogs, will howl for grief.

There is no vice that will not there have its proper torment.

There, the proud will be filled with all confusion, and the covetous be straitened with most miserable want.

There one hour of suffering will be more sharp than a hundred years here spent in the most rigid penance.

There is no rest, no comfort for the damned; but here there is sometimes intermission of labor, and we receive comfort from our friends.

Be careful at present, and sorrowful for your sins: that in the day of judgment, you may be secure with the blessed.

For then, the just shall stand with great constancy against those that afflicted and oppressed them (Wisd. 5:1).

Then will he stand to judge, who now humbly submits himself to the judgment of men. Then, the poor and the humble will have great confidence, and the proud will fear on every side.

Learn at present to suffer little things, that then you may be delivered from more grievous sufferings.

Try first here what you cannot suffer hereafter. If you can now endure so little, how will you be able to bear everlasting torments? If a little suffering now makes you so impatient, what will hellfire do hereafter?

Surely, you cannot have your pleasure in this world and afterward reign with Christ.

On Being Determined to Amend Our Whole Lives
(Thomas à Kempis, *The Imitation of Christ*, book I, chapter 25)

If to this day you had always lived in honors and pleasures, what would it avail you, if you were now in a moment to die?

All then is vanity but to love God and to serve him alone!

For he that loves God with his whole heart neither fears death, nor punishment, nor judgment, nor hell; because perfect love gives secure access to God.

But he that is yet delighted with sin, no wonder if he be afraid of death and judgment. It is good, however, that if love as yet reclaim you not from evil, at least the fear of hell restrain you.

But he that lays aside the fear of God will not be able to continue long in good but will quickly fall into the snares of the devil.

Trust in the Lord, and do good, says the prophet, and inhabit the land, and thou shalt be fed with its riches (Ps. 36:3).

There is one thing that keeps many back from spiritual progress and fervent amendment of life, and that is the apprehension of difficulty or the labor that must be gone through in the conflict.

And they indeed advance most of all others in virtue, who strive manfully to overcome those things that they find more troublesome or contrary to them.

For there, a man makes greater progress and merits greater grace, where he overcomes himself more and mortifies himself in spirit.

But all men have not alike to overcome and mortify.

Yet he that is diligent and zealous, although he have more passions to fight against, will be able to make a greater progress than another who has fewer passions but is withal less fervent in the pursuit of virtue.

Two things particularly conduce to a great amendment: these are, forcibly to withdraw oneself from that to which nature is viciously inclined, and earnestly to labor for that good that one wants the most.

Giving Glory to God in the World

(St. John Henry Newman, *Parochial and Plain Sermons*, volume 8, sermon 11)

When persons are convinced that life is short, that it is unequal to any great purpose, that it does not display adequately, or bring to perfection the true Christian, when they feel that the next life is all in all and that eternity is the only subject that really can claim or can fill their thoughts, then they are apt to undervalue this life altogether and to forget its real importance. They are apt to wish to spend the time of their sojourning here in a positive separation from active and social duties. Yet it should be recollected that the employments of this world, though not themselves heavenly, are, after all, the way to heaven — though not the fruit, are the seed of immortality — and are valuable, though not in themselves, yet for that to which they lead. But it is difficult to realize this. It is difficult to realize both truths at once, and to connect both truths together; steadily to contemplate the life to come, yet to act in this. Those who meditate are likely to neglect those active duties which are, in fact, incumbent on them, and to dwell upon the thought of God's glory, till they forget to act to His glory. This state of mind is chided in figure in the words of the holy angels to the Apostles, when they say, "Men of Galilee, why do you stand looking up to heaven?" (Acts 1:11).

In various ways does the thought of the next world lead men to neglect their duty in this; and whenever it does so, we may be sure that there is something wrong and unchristian, not in their thinking of the next world, but in their manner of thinking of it. For though the contemplation of God's glory may in certain times and persons allowably interfere with the active employments of life, as in the case of the Apostles when our Savior ascended, and though such contemplation is even freely allowed or commanded us at certain times of each day, yet that is not a real and true meditation on Christ, but some counterfeit, which makes us dream away our time, or become habitually indolent, or which withdraws us from our existing duties, or unsettles us.

I am speaking of a case when it is a person's duty to remain in his worldly calling, and when he does remain in it, but when he cherishes dissatisfaction with it, whereas what he ought to feel is this: that while, in it, he is to glorify God—not out of it, but in it, and by means of it, according to the Apostle's direction, "not slothful in zeal; be fervent in spirit, serving the Lord" (Rom.12:11). The Lord Jesus Christ, our Savior, is best served, and with the most fervent spirit, when men are not slothful in business, but do their duty in that state of life in which it has pleased God to call them....

Bad as it is to be languid and indifferent in our secular duties and to account this religion, yet it is far worse to be the slaves of this world and to have our hearts in the concerns of this world.... I mean that ambitious spirit, to use a great word, but I know no other word to express my meaning—that low ambition which sets everyone on the lookout to succeed and to rise in life, to amass money, to gain power, to depress his rivals, to triumph over his hitherto superiors, to affect a consequence and a gentility that he had not before, to affect to have an opinion on high subjects, to pretend to form a judgment upon sacred things, to choose his religion, to approve and condemn according to his taste, to become a partisan in extensive measures for the supposed temporal benefit of the community, to indulge the vision of great things that are to come, great improvements, great wonders: all things vast, all things new. This most fearfully earthly and groveling spirit is likely, alas! to extend itself more and more among our countrymen—an intense, sleepless, restless, never-wearied, never-satisfied pursuit of mammon in one shape or other, to the exclusion of all deep, all holy, all calm, all reverent thoughts. *This* is the spirit in which, more or less (according to their different tempers), men do commonly engage in concerns of this world; and I repeat it, better, far better, were it to retire from the world altogether than thus to engage in it—better with Elijah to fly to the desert, than to serve Baal and Ashtoreth in Jerusalem.

But surely it is possible to "serve the Lord" yet not to be slothful in business; not to be overly devoted to it, but not to retire from it. We may do all things whatever we are about to God's glory; we may do *all things heartily*, as to the Lord, and not to man, being both active yet meditative; and now let me give some instances to show what I mean.

"Do all for the glory of God," says St. Paul; nay, "whether you eat or drink" (1 Cor. 10:31), so that it appears that nothing is too slight or trivial to glory Him in. We will suppose then, to take the case mentioned just now; we will suppose a man who has lately had more serious thoughts than he had before and determines to live more religiously. In consequence of the turn his mind has taken, he feels a distaste for his worldly occupation, whether he is in trade, or in any mechanical employment that allows little exercise of mind. He now feels he would rather be in some other business, though in itself his present occupation is quite lawful and pleasing to God. The ill-instructed man will at once get impatient and quit it; or, if he does not quit it, at least he will be negligent and indolent in it. But the true penitent will say to himself, "No, if it be an irksome employment, so much the more does it suit me. I deserve no better. I do not deserve to be fed even with husks. I am bound to afflict my soul for past sins. If I were to go in sackcloth and ashes, if I were to live on bread and water, if I were to wash the feet of the poor day by day, it would not be too great a humiliation. And the only reason I do not is that I have no call that way; it would look ostentatious. Gladly, then, will I hail an inconvenience that will try me without anyone's knowing it. Far from repining, I will, through God's grace, go cheerfully about what I do not like. I will deny myself. I know that with His help, what is in itself painful will thus be pleasant as done toward Him. I know well that there is no pain but may be borne comfortably, by the thought of Him, and by His grace, and the strong determination of the will; nay, none but may soothe and solace me. Even the natural taste and smell may be made to like what they naturally dislike; even bitter medicine, which is nauseous to the palate, may by a resolute will become tolerable. Nay, even sufferings and torture, such as martyrs have borne, have before now been rejoiced in and embraced heartily from love to Christ. I, then, a sinner, will take this light inconvenience in a generous way, pleased at the opportunity of disciplining myself, and with self-abasement, as needing a severe penitence. If there be parts in my occupation that I especially dislike, if it requires a good deal of moving about, and I wish to be at home; or if it be sedentary, and I wish to be in motion; or if it requires rising early, and I like to rise late; or if it makes me solitary, and I like to be with friends, all this unpleasant part, as far as is consistent with my health, and so that it is not likely to be a snare to me, I will choose by preference.

Again, I see my religious views are a hindrance to me. I see persons are suspicious of me. I see that I offend people by my scrupulousness. I see that to get on in life requires far more devotion to my worldly business than I can give consistently with my duty to God, or without it becoming a temptation to me. I know that I ought not, and (please God) I will not, sacrifice my religion to it. My religious seasons and hours shall be my own. I will not countenance any of the worldly dealings and practices, the overreaching ways, the sordid actions in which others indulge.

And if I am thrown back in life thereby, if I make fewer gains or lose friends, and so come to be despised, and find others rise in the world while I remain where I was, hard though this be to bear, it is a humiliation that becomes me in requital for my sins, and in obedience to God; and a very slight one it is, merely to be deprived of worldly successes, or rather, it is a gain. And this may be the manner in which Almighty God will make an opening for me, if it is His blessed will, to leave my present occupation. But leave it without a call from God, I certainly must not.

On the contrary, I will work in it, the more diligently as far as higher duties allow me.

Thankfulness to Almighty God, nay, and the inward life of the Spirit itself will be additional principles causing the Christian to labor diligently in his calling. He will see God in all things. He will recollect our Savior's life. Christ was brought up to a humble trade. When the Christian labors in his own, he will think of his Lord and Master in His. He will recollect that Christ went down to Nazareth and was subject to His parents, that He walked long journeys, that He bore the sun's heat and the storm and had nowhere to lay His head. Again, he knows that the Apostles had various employments before their calling; St. Andrew and St. Peter were fishers, St. Matthew a tax gatherer, and St. Paul, even after his calling, was still a tent maker. Accordingly, in whatever comes upon him, he will endeavor to discern and gaze (as it were) on the countenance of his Savior. He will feel that the true contemplation of that Savior lies in his worldly business; that as Christ is seen in the poor, and in the persecuted, and in children, so is He seen in the employments that He puts upon His chosen, whatever they be; that in attending to his own calling, he will be meeting Christ; that if he neglects it, he will not on that account enjoy His presence at all the more, but that while performing it, he will see Christ revealed to his soul amid the ordinary actions of the day, as by a sort of sacrament. Thus, he will take his worldly business as a gift from Him and will love it as such.

Still further, he will use his worldly business as a means of keeping him from vain and unprofitable thoughts. One cause of the heart's devising evil is that time is given it to do so. The man who has his daily duties, who lays out his time for them hour by hour, is saved a multitude of sins that have not time to get hold upon him. The brooding over insults received, or the longing after some good not granted, or regret at losses that have befallen us, or at the loss of friends by death, or the attacks of impure and shameful thoughts: these are kept off him who takes care to be diligent and well employed. Leisure is the occasion of all evil. Idleness is the first step in the downward path that leads to hell. If we do not find employment to engage our minds with, Satan will be sure to find his own employment for them.

Here we see the differences of motive with which a religious and a worldly-minded man may do the same thing. Suppose a person has had some sad affliction, say, a bereavement. Men of this world, having no pleasure in religion, not liking to dwell on a loss to them irreparable, in order to drown reflection, betake themselves to worldly pursuits to divert their thoughts and banish gloom. The Christian, under the same circumstances, does the same thing, but it is from a fear lest he should relax and enfeeble his mind by barren sorrow; from a dread of becoming discontented; from a belief that he is pleasing God better, and is likely to secure his peace more fully, by not losing time; from a feeling that, far from forgetting those whom he has lost by thus acting, he shall only enjoy the thought of them the more really and the more religiously.

Lastly, we see what judgment to give in a question sometimes agitated, whether one should retire from our worldly business at the close of life, to give our thoughts more entirely to God. To wish to do so is so natural that I suppose there is no one who would not wish it. A great many persons are not allowed the privilege, a great many are allowed it through increasing infirmities or extreme old age; but everyone, I conceive, if allowed to choose, would think it a privilege to be allowed it, though a great many would find it difficult to determine when was the fit time. But let us consider what is the reason of this so natural a wish. I fear that it is often not a religious wish, often only partially religious. I fear a great number of persons who whim at retiring from the world's business, do so under the notion of their then enjoying themselves somewhat after the manner of the rich man in the Gospel, who said, "Soul, thou hast many good things laid up for many years" (Luke 12:19). If this is the predominant aim of anyone, of course, I need not say that it is a fatal sin, for Christ Himself has said so (Luke 12:20). Others there are who are actuated by a mixed feeling; they are aware that they do not give so much time to religion as they ought; they do not live by rule; nay, they are not satisfied with the correctness or uprightness of some of the practices or customs that their way of life requires of them, and they get tired of active business as life goes on, and wish to be at ease. So they look to their last years as a time of retirement, in which they may both enjoy themselves and prepare for heaven. And thus, they satisfy both their conscience and their love of the world. At present, religion is irksome to them; but then, as they hope, duty and pleasure will go together.

Now, putting aside all other mistakes which such a frame of mind evidences, let it be observed that if they are at present not serving God with all their hearts, but look forward to a time when they shall do so, then it is plain that when at length they do put aside worldly cares and turn to God, if ever they do, that time must necessarily be a time of deep humiliation, if it is to be acceptable to Him, not a comfortable retirement. Whoever heard of a pleasurable, easy, joyous repentance? It is a contradiction in terms. These men, if they do but reflect a moment, must confess that their present mode of life, supposing it be not so strict as it should be, is heaping up tears and groans for their last years, not enjoyment. The longer they live as they do at present, not only the more unlikely is it that they will repent at all; but even if they do, the more bitter, the more painful must their repentance be. The only way to escape suffering for sin hereafter is to suffer for it here. Sorrow here or misery hereafter; they cannot escape one or the other.

Not for any worldly reason, then, not on presumptuous or unbelieving motive, does the Christian desire leisure and retirement for his last years. Nay, he will be content to do with these blessings, and the highest Christian of all is he whose heart is so stayed on God that he does not wish or need it; whose heart is so set on things above that things below as little excite, agitate, unsettle, distress, and seduce him as they stop the course of nature, as they stop the sun and moon or change summer and winter. Such were the Apostles, who, as the heavenly bodies, went out to "all nations" full of business, and yet full, too, of sweet harmony, even to the ends of the earth. Their calling was heavenly, but their work was earthly; they were in labor and trouble till the last, yet consider how calmly St. Paul and St. Peter write in their last days. St. John, on the other hand, was allowed, in a great measure, to retire from the cares of his pastoral charge, and such, I say, will be the natural wish of every religious man, whether his ministry be spiritual or secular; but, not in order to begin to fix his mind on God, but merely because, though he may contemplate God as truly and be as holy in heart in active business as in quiet, still it is more becoming and suitable to meet the stroke of death (if it be allowed us) silently, collectively, solemnly, than in a crowd and a tumult. And hence it is, among other reasons, that we pray in the Litany to be delivered "from *sudden* death."

On the whole, then, what I have said comes to this, that whereas Adam was sentenced to labor as a punishment, Christ has by His coming sanctified it as means of grace and a sacrifice of thanksgiving, a sacrifice cheerfully to be offered up to the Father in His name.

May God give us grace in our several spheres and stations to do His will and adorn His doctrine; that whether we eat and drink, or fast and pray, labor with our hands or with our minds, journey about or remain at rest, we may glorify Him who has purchased us with His own blood!

Prayer in the Storms of Life
(From *The Raccolta*)

Thou seest, O Lord, how on all sides the winds are let loose upon us, and the sea is growing rough with the violent commotion of the waves. Do thou, we beseech Thee, who alone art able, command the winds and the waves. Restore to mankind that true peace which the world cannot give, the peace which comes of good order. Let men, impelled by Thy grace, return to a right and orderly course of life, practicing again, as they ought, love toward God, justice, and charity in dealing with their neighbor, temperance and self-control in their own lives. May Thy kingdom come, and may those who now vainly and laboriously seek for truth and salvation, far removed from Thee, understand that they must live as Thy servants in subjection to Thee. Thy laws show forth Thy justice and paternal gentleness, and to enable us to keep them, Thou dost freely supply by Thy grace the ready means. The life of man on earth is a warfare, but "Thou dost Thyself behold the strife, Thou dost help man to conquer, raise him when he falls, and crown him when he is victorious."

A Prayer That God's Will May Be Done
(Thomas à Kempis, *The Imitation of Christ*, book 3, chapter 15)

Grant me Your grace, most merciful Jesus, that it may be with me, and continue with me to the end.

Grant me always to will and desire that which is most acceptable to You and pleases You best.

Let Your will be mine, and let my will always follow Yours, and agree perfectly with it.

Let me always will or not will the same with You: and let me not be able to will or not will otherwise than as You will or will not.

Grant that I may die to all things that are in the world and, for Your sake, love to be despised and not to be known in this world.

Grant that I may rest in You above all things desired and that my heart may be at peace in You.

You are the true peace of heart; You are its only rest: outside of You, all things are hard and uneasy.

"In this peace, in the self-same that is in thee, the one sovereign, eternal God, I will sleep, and I will rest" (Ps. 4:9). Amen.

We Are Not to Trust in Men, but in God Alone

Praise the Lord, O my soul, in my life I will praise the Lord: I will sing to my God as long as I shall be. Put not your trust in princes:

In the children of men, in whom there is no salvation.

His spirit shall go forth, and he shall return into his earth: in that day all their thoughts shall perish.

Blessed is he who hath the God of Jacob for his helper, whose hope is in the Lord his God:

Who made heaven and earth, the sea, and all things that are in them.

Who keepeth truth for ever: who executeth judgment for them that suffer wrong: who giveth food to the hungry. The Lord looseth them that are fettered:

The Lord enlighteneth the blind. The Lord lifteth up them that are cast down: the Lord loveth the just.

The Lord keepeth the strangers, he will support the fatherless and the widow: and the ways of sinners he will destroy.

The Lord shall reign for ever: thy God, O Sion, unto generation and generation. (Ps. 145)

Sixth Meditation

The Eucharist, the Need of Our Heart

(From St. Peter Julian Eymard, *The Real Presence*)

[Why is Jesus Christ in the Eucharist?] We might make several answers to this question. But that which comprises them all is this: He is there because He loves us, and because He desires that we love Him. Love — that is the reason of the institution of the Eucharist.

Without the Eucharist, the love of Jesus Christ would be for us a dead love, a past love, that we should soon forget and should be almost pardonable in forgetting. Love has its laws, its demands. The Eucharist alone fully satisfies them. By it, Jesus Christ has every right to be loved, because He testifies in the Eucharist to His infinite love for us.

Now, natural love, such as God has put into our hearts, demands three things: the presence of the loved one, or social life; community of goods; and perfect union.

Absence is the pain of friendship, its torment. Distance weakens and, if it is too prolonged, ends the firmest friendship by putting it to death.

If Our Lord is away from us, removed from us, our love for Him will undergo the dissolving effect of absence. It is in the nature of man's love to require, in order to live, the presence of the object loved.

Behold the poor Apostles while Our Lord was in the tomb. The disciples of Emmaus avowed that they had almost lost faith because they no longer had their good Master.

Ah! If Our Lord had left us with no other pledge of His Love than Bethlehem and Calvary—poor Savior! How quickly we would have forgotten Him! What indifference! Love wishes to see, to hear, to converse, to touch.

Nothing takes the place of the beloved one, neither souvenir, nor gifts, nor portraits. All that is without life.

Our Lord knew it well. Nothing could have taken the place of His Person. We need Our Lord Himself.

But His Word? No, it no longer sounds. We no longer hear the touching accents that fell from the lips of the Savior.

His Gospel? It is a testament.

But His sacraments—do they not give life? Ah! it takes the Author of life to sustain it in us!

The Cross? No; apart from Jesus, it only saddens!

"But hope? Without Jesus, it is agony! . . .

Could Jesus have wished to reduce us to so sad a state of living and struggling without Him?

Oh, we would be too unhappy without Jesus present with us! Exiled, alone upon earth, obliged to deprive ourselves of terrestrial goods, of the consolations of life, while the worldling has all that he desires—life would be insupportable!

But with the Eucharist! With Jesus in the midst of us ... by day and by night, accessible to all, waiting for everyone in His ever-open house, admitting the lowly, calling them with marked predilection—ah! Life is less bitter. He is the good Father in the midst of His children. It is social life with Jesus.

And what society! Society that makes us better, that elevates us! And what facilities for social relations with heaven, with Jesus Christ Himself in person! It is, indeed, the sweet companionship of simple, loving, familiar, and intimate friendship.

Ah! It was necessary!

Love desires community of goods, common possession. It wishes to share happiness and unhappiness. To give is its nature, its instinct, to give all with joy, with pleasure. And so, Jesus Christ, in the Most Blessed Sacrament, gives with profusion, with prodigality, His merits, His graces, yes, even His glory! Oh, how eager He is to give! He never refuses.

And He gives Himself to all, and always.

He covers the world with consecrated Hosts. He wishes all His children to possess Him. There still remain twelve baskets of the five loaves multiplied in the desert. All must have some!

Jesus Christ would wish to envelop the world in His sacramental veil, to fertilize all nations in the waters of life that are losing themselves in the ocean of eternity, but only after having slaked the thirst, and strengthened the last of the elect.

Ah! it is well for us, for all of us, O Eucharistic Jesus!

Love tends to union, the union of those who love, the fusion of two into one, of two hearts into one heart, of two spirits into one, of two souls into one....

Jesus submitted to this law of love, which He had Himself established. After having shared our state, our life, He gives Himself in Communion; He absorbs us into Himself.

Divine union of souls, always more perfect, always more intimate in proportion to the vivacity of our desires! *In me manet, et ego in eo.* — *He in me, and I in Him.* We abide in Him; He dwells in us. We make but one with Him until heaven consummates in eternal and glorious union the ineffable union commenced here below by grace, and perfected by the Eucharist!

Love lives, then, with Jesus present in the Most Blessed Sacrament. It shares all the riches of Jesus. It is united with Jesus.

The needs of our heart are satisfied. It can demand no more.

We believe in the love of God for us: words of deep significance!

Faith in the truth of the divine words and promises is exacted of every Christian. That is simply faith. But the faith of love is higher and more perfect. It is the crown of the first.

Faith in truth would be sterile if it did not lead to faith in love.

What is that love in which we ought to believe?

141

It is the love of Jesus Christ, the love that He testifies to us in the Eucharist, the love that is Himself, living and infinite love. Happy they who believe in the love of Jesus Christ in the Eucharist! They love, for to believe is to love.

They who are satisfied with believing in the truth of the Eucharist love not at all or love very little. But what proofs of His love has Our Lord given in the Eucharist? In the first place, Our Lord has given us His word to that effect. He tells us that He loves us, that He has instituted His Sacrament only for love of us. Then it is true.

We believe an honorable man on his word. Why should we put less faith in that of Our Lord? When a friend desires to prove to his friend that he loves him, he tells him so, and he presses his hand affectionately. When Our Lord wants to show His love for us, He does so in person, discarding the intervention of any third person, whether angelic or human. Love suffers no intermediate agents.

He remains in the Holy Eucharist that He may repeat to us incessantly: "I love you! You must see that I love you!"

Our Lord was so afraid that we would eventually forget Him that He took up His abode in the midst of us, made His home among us, placed His service within our reach, so that we might not be able to think of Him without calling to mind His love. Giving Himself thus, He hoped, perhaps, not to be forgotten by men.

Whoever reflects seriously on the Eucharist, but, above all, whoever participates in it, must feel convinced that Our Lord loves him. He feels that he has in Him a Father. He feels that he is loved as a child. He feels that he has the right to go to Him as to a Father and to speak freely with him. When in church, at the foot of the tabernacle, he is at home with his Father. He feels it.

Ah! I understand why the faithful love to live near churches, under the shadow of the paternal home.

Thus, Jesus, in the Most Blessed Sacrament, tells us that He loves us. He repeats it to us interiorly and makes us feel it. Let us believe in His love.

Does Jesus love us personally, individually? To this question, there is but one answer: Do we belong to the Christian family? In a family, do not the father and the mother love each child with equal love? And if they had some preference, would it not be for the most delicate or infirm?

Our Lord has for us the sentiment, at least, of a good Father. Why do we refuse Him that character?

But still more, see how Our Lord exercises toward each one of us His personal love. He comes every morning to see each of His children, in particular, to visit, speak to, and embrace each one. Although He comes so often, His visit is always as gracious, as loving as if it were the very first. He has not grown old. He is never tired of loving us, and of giving Himself to each of us.

Does He not give Himself whole and entire to each one? And if the communicants are more numerous than the Hosts, does He not divide Himself for them? Does He ever give less to anyone?

Even if the church is filled with adorers, cannot each one of us pray to Jesus, converse with Him? And is one not heard, is one not answered as favorably, as if he were alone in the church?

Such is the personal love of Jesus. Everyone receives Him entire and does no wrong to anyone. As the sun sheds its light on each and all, as the ocean belongs entirely to each and all the fishes, so does Jesus belong to all of us. He is greater than all. He is inexhaustible.

Another undeniable proof of the love of Our Lord is the persistence of that love in the Most Blessed Sacrament.

How touching is this thought to the soul that understands! Numberless Masses are daily celebrated all over the world. They succeed one another almost without interruption. And how many of these Masses, in which Jesus offers Himself for us, are unattended, how many without assistants? While, on this new Calvary, Jesus is crying for mercy, sinners are outraging God and His Christ.

Why does Our Lord renew His sacrifices so often, since we do not profit by it? Why does He remain day and night on our altars, to which no one comes to receive the graces that He is offering with full hands?

Because He is loving, He is hoping, He is expecting! If Jesus came on our altars only on certain days, He would fear that some sinner, impelled by a desire to return to Him, might come seeking Him and, not finding Him, would go away without waiting for Him. So, He prefers to await the sinner for long years Himself rather than make him wait an instant, rather than discourage him, perhaps, when he wants to escape from the slavery of sin.

Oh, how few have even a remote idea of the love of Jesus in the Most Blessed Sacrament! And, nevertheless, it is true! Oh, we have no faith in the love of Jesus! Would we treat a friend, would we treat any man, as we do Our Lord?

The Devout Soul Should Long Wholeheartedly for Union with Christ in the Sacrament
(Thomas à Kempis, *The Imitation of Christ*, book 4, chapter 13)

Who will give me, O Lord, to find You alone, that I may open my whole heart to You and enjoy You as my soul desires; no one beholding me, nor any creature interesting me, or at all affecting me, but You alone speaking to me, and I to You, as the beloved is wont to speak to his beloved, and a friend to entertain himself with his friend.

This I pray for, this I desire, that I may be wholly united to You, and may withdraw my heart from all created things; and through Holy Communion ... may more and more learn to relish heavenly and eternal things.

Ah! Lord God, when shall I be wholly united to and absorbed in You, and altogether forgetful of myself? You in me and I in you; and so grant us both to continue in one.

Verily, You are my Beloved, the choicest among thousands, in whom my soul is well pleased to dwell all the days of my life.

Verily, You are my Peacemaker, in whom is sovereign peace and true rest; without whom is labor, and sorrow, and endless misery.

You are, in truth, a hidden God, and Your counsel is not with the wicked; but Your conversation is with the humble and the simple.

Oh! how sweet is Your spirit, O Lord, who, to show Your sweetness toward your children, vouchsafe to feed them with the most delicious bread, which comes down from heaven.

Surely there is no other nation so great that has their God so near to them, as You, our God, are present to Your faithful; to whom, for their daily comfort and for the raising of their hearts to heaven, You give yourself to be eaten and enjoyed.

For what other nation is there so honored as the Christian people? Or what creature under heaven so beloved as a devout soul, into whom God comes, that He may feed him with His glorious Flesh? O unspeakable grace! O wonderful condescension!

O, infinite love, singularly bestowed upon man!

But what return shall I make to the Lord for this grace, and for so extraordinary a charity?

There is nothing that I can give Him that will please Him better than if I give my heart entirely to God and unite it closely to Him.

Then all that is within me shall rejoice exceedingly, when my soul shall be perfectly united to my God; then will He say to me: "If you will be with me, I will be with you"; and I will answer Him: "Vouchsafe, O Lord, to remain with me, and I will willingly be with You."

This is my whole desire: that my heart may be united to You.

Seventh Meditation

Our Blessed Mother

Certain modern forms of Christianity speak of the Babe but never a word about the Mother of the Babe. The Babe of Bethlehem did not fall from the heavens into a bed of straw but came into this world through the great portals of the flesh. Sons are inseparable from mothers, and mothers are inseparable from sons. Just as you cannot go to a statue of a mother holding a babe and cut away the mother, leaving the babe suspended in midair, neither can you cleave away the Mother from the Babe of Bethlehem. He was not suspended in midair in history, but, like all other babes, came into the world by and through His Mother. While we adore the Child, should we not then venerate His Mother, and while we kneel to Jesus, should we not at least clasp the hand of Mary for giving us such a Savior? There is a grave danger that, in celebrating Christmas without the Mother, we may soon reach a point where we will celebrate Christmas without the Babe, and these days are upon us now. And what an absurdity that is; for, just as there can never be a Christmas without a Christ, so there can never be a Christ without a Mary. Pull aside the curtain of the past, and under the light of Revelation, discover the role and interpret the part that Mary plays in the great drama of redemption!

Almighty God never launches a great work without exceeding preparation. The two greatest works of God are the creation of the first man, Adam, and the Incarnation of the Son of God, the new Adam, Jesus

Christ. But neither of these was accomplished without characteristic divine preparation.

God did not make the masterpiece of creation, which was man, on the very first day, but deferred it until He had labored for six days in ornamenting the universe. From no material thing, but only by the fiat of His will, Omnipotence moved and said to nothingness, "Be"; and lo and behold, spheres fell into their orbits, passing one another in beautiful harmony, without ever a hitch or a halt. Then came the living things: the herbs bearing fruit as unconscious tribute to their Maker; the trees, with their leafy arms, outstretched all day in prayer; and the flowers, opening the chalice of their perfumes to their Creator. With the labor that was never exhausting, God then made the sensitive creatures to roam about, either in the watery palaces of the depths or on wings to fly through trackless space, or else, as unwinged, to roam the field in search of their repast and natural happiness. But all of this beauty, which has inspired the song of poets and the tracings of artists, was not in the Divine Mind sufficiently beautiful for the creature whom God would make the lord and master of the universe. He would do one thing more: He would set apart as a choice garden a small portion of His creation, beautify it with four rivers flowing through lands rich with gold and onyx, and permit to roam in it the beasts of the field as domestics of that garden, in order to make it a paradise of the most intense happiness and pleasure possible to earth. When finally that Eden was made beautiful, as only God knows how to make things beautiful, He launched further the masterpiece of His creation, which was the first man, and in that paradise of pleasure was celebrated the first nuptials of humanity—the union of flesh and flesh of the first man and woman, Adam and Eve.

Now, if God so prepared for His first great work, which was man, by making the paradise of Creation, it was even more fitting that before sending His Son to redeem the world, He should prepare for Him a paradise of the Incarnation. And for many long centuries, He prepared it by symbols and prophecies. In the language of types, He prepared human minds for some understanding of what this new paradise would be. The burning bush of Moses, inundated with the glory of God and conserving in the midst of its flame the freshness of its verdure and the perfume of its flowers, was a symbol of a new paradise, conserving in the honor of its maturity the very perfume of virginity. The rod of Aaron, flourishing in the solitude of the Temple while isolated from the world by silence and retreat, was a symbol of the paradise that, in a place of retirement and isolation from the world, would engender the very flower of the human race. The Ark of alliance, where the tablets of the Law were conserved, was a symbol of the new paradise in which the Law in the Person of Christ would take up His very residence.

God prepared for that paradise, not only by symbols but also by prophecies. Even in that dread day when an angel with a flaming sword was stationed in the first garden in creation, a prophecy was made that the serpent would not eventually conquer, but that a woman would crush its head. Later on, Isaiah and Jeremiah hailed that holy paradise as one that would encircle a man.

But prophets and symbols were a too-distant preparation. God would labor still more on His paradise. He would make a paradise not overrun with weeds and thistles, but blooming with every flower of virtue; a paradise at the portals of which sin had never knocked, against the gates of which infidelity would never dare to storm; a paradise from which would flow not four rivers through lands rich with gold and onyx, but four oceans of grace to the four corners of the world; a paradise destined to bring forth the Tree of Life, and, therefore, full of life and grace itself; a paradise in which was to be tabernacled Purity itself, and therefore one immaculately pure; a paradise so beautiful and sublime that the heavenly Father would not have to blush in sending His Son into it. That flesh-gift paradise of the Incarnation in which there were to be celebrated the nuptials, not of man and woman, but of humanity and divinity, is our own beloved Mary, Mother of Our Lord and Savior, Jesus Christ.

Why should not that paradise of the Incarnation be spotless and pure? Why should she not be immaculate and stainless? Just suppose that you could have preexisted your mother, in much the same way that an artist preexists his painting. Furthermore, suppose that you had an infinite power to make your mother anything that you pleased, just as a great artist such as Raphael has the power of realizing his artistic ideals. Suppose you had this double power. What kind of mother would you have made for yourself? Would you have made her of such a type that would make you blush because of her unwomanly and unmotherlike actions? Would you have in any way stained and soiled her with the selfishness that would make her unattractive not only to you but to your fellow man? Would you have made her exteriorly and interiorly of such a character as to make you ashamed of her? Or would you have made her, so far as human beauty goes, the most beautiful woman in the world; and so far as beauty of soul goes, one who would radiate every virtue, every manner of kindness and charity and loveliness; one who by the purity of her life and her mind and her heart would be an inspiration not only to you but even to your fellow men, so that all would look up to her as the very incarnation of what is best in motherhood?

Now, if you, who are an imperfect being and who have not the most delicate conception of all that is fine in life, would have wished for the loveliest of mothers, do you think that our Blessed Lord, who not only preexisted His mother but who had an infinite power to make her just what He chose, would, in virtue of all of the infinite delicacy of His spirit, make her any less pure and loving and beautiful than you would have made your own mother? If you who hate selfishness and ugliness, would have made her beautiful, do you not think that the Son of God, who hates sin, would have made His own mother sinless, and He who hates moral ugliness would have made her immaculately beautiful?

Note how Sacred Scripture first implicitly and then explicitly reveals how Mary is the Mother of Christians. St. Luke, in recounting the birth of Our Lord, says that Mary brought forth her "firstborn." Certain critics have argued that this meant our Blessed Mother had other children according to the flesh, although, in fact, the Scriptures clearly indicate she was a virgin. The term *firstborn* may indeed mean that Mary was to have other children, not by the flesh but by the Spirit. It suggests that she was to have a spiritual progeny, which would make up the Mystical Body of her Divine Son, just as Eve is called the "mother of all living" or the mother of men in the natural order. Sara gave only one son to the father of believers, Abraham, and yet she is called the mother of all Israel. There is a clear suggestion in the word *firstborn* that she who begot corporally the Head of the Church was also to beget spiritually the members of the Church. Since the Head and the Body are inseparable, it is, therefore, true to say that as Mary bore Christ in her womb, she was virtually carrying the whole Mystical Body. The mother earth that bears the vine also bears the branches.

When finally the Word is made flesh, and she brings Him to the Temple on the fortieth day for purification, Mary's role in the Redemption becomes even clearer. Joseph was with her on that day, but the aged Simeon spoke only to her and reminded her that she was pierced by the sword of sorrow. Simeon, full of the prophetic spirit, was looking forward to the day when this Babe, the new Adam, would atone for sin on the Cross, as the Man of Sorrows, and where she, as the new Eve, would cooperate in that Redemption as the Woman of Sorrows. Simeon was practically telling her that Eden would become Calvary, the tree would be the Cross, and she would be the Mother of the Redeemer. But if she is the Mother of the Redeemer, then was she not called to be the Mother of the Redeemed? And if Christ was her firstborn, would not the Redeemed be her other born, brothers of Christ and sons of the heavenly Father?

All this became clearer when Our Lord began to preach. One day, as He was breaking the bread of truth to the multitude, someone in the crowd announced that His Blessed Mother was seeking Him. "But he answered and said unto him who told him, 'Who is my mother ...?' And, stretching forth his hand towards his disciples, he said, 'Behold my mother and my brethren! For whoever does the will of my Father in heaven, he is my brother and sister and mother'" (Matt. 12:48–50, KJV). These words did not mean a denial of His Blessed Mother, whom He loved next to His own heavenly Father; rather did they mean that there are other ties than those of the flesh. The world was being prepared for the fuller and deeper significance of the word *firstborn*. That day came on the Friday called Good and on a hill called Calvary. Our Lord had already given His garments to His executioners. Later on, He was to give His body to the grave, and His Spirit to His Father. But He has two precious gifts yet to be conferred: His beloved disciple John and His sorrowful Mother, Mary. To whom could He give such gifts except to each other? And so to John, as representative of beloved redeemed humanity, He said: "Behold thy Mother." Then, looking to His Mother, He said—not "Mother," but "Woman," to remind her of her universal relation to the race of the Redeemer—"Woman, behold thy son." "Behold thy son"—she had one Son already; He was hanging on the tree of ignominy. Now she was to have another, a son of Zebedee. John, then, was her second born!

All becomes clear. Her Son told her there was another motherhood, besides that of the flesh; now she realizes how literally true it was that she brought forth her firstborn in Bethlehem, and His name is Jesus; she brings forth her second born on Calvary. Mary was destined to have children other than Jesus, but they were to be born not of her flesh but of her heart. Mother of Christ was she at the Cross. Her firstborn in Bethlehem was brought forth in joy, but the curse of Eve hung about her labors at the Cross, for she was now, like Eve, bringing forth her children in sorrow. At that moment, Mary suffered the pangs of spiritual child-birth for the millions of souls who would ever be called to the adoptive sonship of the Father, the brotherhood of Christ, and the joy of calling her Mother. The cup of her sorrow at the Cross, like her Son's, was filled to the brim, and no one knows how much she suffered to become our spiritual Mother or the Mother of the Mystical Body of her Divine Son. We know only that the millions of martyrs throughout all Christian ages consider their pains as insignificant compared with hers and scruple not to address her as the Queen of Martyrs.

If Our Savior could have thought of any better means of leading us back to Him, He would have put us in other hands than hers.

There are many falsehoods told about the Catholic Church. One of them is that Catholics adore Mary. This is absolutely untrue. Mary is a creature, human, not divine. Catholics do not adore Mary. That would be idolatry. But they do reverence her.

And to those Christians who have forgotten Mary, may we ask if it is proper for them to forget her whom He remembered on the Cross? Will they bear no love for that woman through the portals of whose flesh, as the gate of heaven, He came to earth?

One of the reasons so many Christians have lost a belief in the divinity of Christ is because they lost all affection for her upon whose white body, as a tower of ivory, that Infant climbed "to kiss upon her lips a mystic rose."

There is not a Christian in all the world who reverences Mary who does not acknowledge Jesus, her Son, to be in truth the Son of the living God. The prudent Christ on the Cross knew the prudent way to preserve belief in His divinity, for who better than a Mother knows her Son?

The gift of Mary did something to man, for it gave him an ideal love.

There has hardly ever been a mother in the history of the world who did not at one time or another say to her son or daughter: "Never do anything of which your mother would be ashamed."

The nobler the love, the nobler the character; and what nobler love could be given to men than the woman whom the Savior of the world chose as His own Mother?

Why is it that the world has confessed its inability to inculcate virtue in the young? Very simply because it has not correlated morality to any love nobler than self-love. Things keep their proportion and fulfill their proper role only when integrated into a larger whole.

Most lives are like doors without hinges, or sleeves without coats, or bows without violins—that is, unrelated to wholes or purposes which give them meaning.

The modern emphasis on sex is a result of tearing a function away from a purpose, a part away from a whole. It can never be handled properly unless integrated into a larger pattern and made to serve it.

That is, to some extent, the role Our Blessed Mother plays in the moral life of our Catholic youth. She is that ideal love for which lesser and baser loves and impulses are sacrificed.

The level of any civilization is the level of its womanhood. What they are, men will be, for love always goes out to meet the demands of the object loved. Given a woman like the Mother of Our Lord as our supernatural Mother, we have one of the greatest inspirations for nobler living this world has ever known.

Salve Regina

Hail Holy Queen, Mother of Mercy. Hail our life, our sweetness, and our hope! To thee do we cry, poor banished children of Eve; to thee do we send up our sighs, mourning, and weeping in this vale of tears. Turn, then, most gracious advocate, thine eyes of mercy toward us; and after this our exile, show unto us the blessed fruit of thy womb, Jesus. O clement, O loving, O sweet Virgin Mary. Pray for us, O holy Mother of God, that we may be made worthy of the promises of Christ. Amen.

Hail Mary

Hail Mary, full of grace, the Lord is with thee. Blessed art thou among women, and blessed is the fruit of thy womb, Jesus. Holy Mary, Mother of God, pray for us sinners, now and at the hour of our death. Amen.

Litany of the Blessed Virgin Mary

Lord, have mercy on us.
Christ, have mercy on us.
Lord, have mercy on us.
Christ, hear us.
Christ, graciously hear us.
God the Father of heaven, *have mercy on us.*
God the Son, Redeemer of the world, *have mercy on us.*

God, the Holy Spirit, *have mercy on us.*
Holy Trinity, one God, *have mercy on us.*
Holy Mary, *pray for us.*
Holy Mother of God, *pray for us.*
Holy Virgin of virgins, *pray for us.*
Mother of Christ, *pray for us.*
Mother of divine grace, *pray for us.*
Mother most pure, *pray for us.*
Mother most chaste, *pray for us.*
Mother inviolate, *pray for us.*
Mother undefiled, *pray for us.*
Mother most amiable, *pray for us.*
Mother most admirable, *pray for us.*
Mother of good counsel, *pray for us.*
Mother of our Creator, *pray for us.*
Mother of our Savior, *pray for us.*
Virgin most prudent, *pray for us.*
Virgin most venerable, *pray for us.*
Virgin most renowned, *pray for us.*
Virgin most powerful, *pray for us.*
Virgin most merciful, *pray for us.*
Virgin most faithful, *pray for us.*
Mirror of justice, *pray for us.*
Seat of wisdom, *pray for us.*
Cause of our joy, *pray for us.*
Spiritual vessel, *pray for us.*
Vessel of honor, *pray for us.*
Singular vessel of devotion, *pray for us.*
Mystical Rose, *pray for us.*
Tower of David, *pray for us.*
Tower of ivory, *pray for us.*
House of gold, *pray for us.*
Ark of the covenant, *pray for us.*

Gate of heaven, *pray for us.*
Morning star, *pray for us.*
Health of the sick, *pray for us.*
Refuge of sinners, *pray for us.*
Comforter of the afflicted, *pray for us.*
Help of Christians, *pray for us.*
Queen of angels, *pray for us.*
Queen of patriarchs, *pray for us.*
Queen of prophets, *pray for us.*
Queen of apostles, *pray for us.*
Queen of martyrs, *pray for us.*
Queen of confessors, *pray for us.*
Queen of virgins, *pray for us.*
Queen of all saints, *pray for us.*
Queen conceived without original sin, *pray for us.*
Queen of the most holy Rosary, *pray for us.*
Queen of peace, *pray for us.*
Lamb of God, who takes away the sins of the world,
spare us, O Lord.
Lamb of God, who takes away the sins of the world,
graciously hear us, O Lord.
Lamb of God, who takes away the sins of the world,
have mercy on us.
Christ, hear us.
Christ, graciously hear us.
Pray for us, O holy Mother of God.
That we may be made worthy of the promises of Christ.

Let us pray: Pour forth, we beseech Thee, O Lord, Thy grace
into our hearts; that we to whom the incarnation of Christ Thy
Son was made known by the message of an angel, may by His
Passion and Cross be brought to the glory of His Resurrection.
Through the same Christ Our Lord.

May the divine assistance remain always with us.
May the souls of the faithful departed, through the mercy of
God, rest in peace. Amen.

We fly to thy patronage, O holy Mother of God. Despise not
our petitions in our necessities, but deliver us from all dangers,
O ever glorious and blessed Virgin. Amen.

4

The Stations of the Cross

(from *The Armor of God*)

This holy devotion commemorates the various incidents that occurred during Our Lord's painful journey with His Cross from the tribunal of Pilate to the hill of Calvary.

First Station:
Jesus is condemned to death.

V. We adore Thee, O Christ, and we bless Thee,
R. Because by Thy holy Cross, Thou hast redeemed the world.

Jesus, when condemned, is silent. How do I act when censured?
Pray the Our Father, the Hail Mary, and the Glory Be.

Second Station:
Jesus bears His Cross.

V. We adore Thee, O Christ, and we bless Thee,
R. Because by Thy holy Cross, Thou hast redeemed the world.

Do I bear my crosses in union with the Cross of Christ?
Pray the Our Father, the Hail Mary, and the Glory Be.

Third Station:
Jesus falls the first time.

V. We adore Thee, O Christ, and we bless Thee,
R. Because by Thy holy Cross, Thou hast redeemed the world.

It is the weight of my sins that caused Jesus to fall.
   Pray the Our Father, the Hail Mary, and the Glory Be.

Fourth Station:
Jesus meets His afflicted Mother.

V. We adore Thee, O Christ, and we bless Thee,
R. Because by Thy holy Cross, Thou hast redeemed the world.

Is my devotion to the Mother of Christ all it should be?
   Pray the Our Father, the Hail Mary, and the Glory Be.

Fifth Station:
The Cyrenian helps Jesus carry His Cross.

V. We adore Thee, O Christ, and we bless Thee,
R. Because by Thy holy Cross, Thou hast redeemed the world.

Unlike Simon, I am unwilling to bear the Cross with Jesus.
   Pray the Our Father, the Hail Mary, and the Glory Be.

Sixth Station:
Veronica wipes the face of Jesus.

V. We adore Thee, O Christ, and we bless Thee,
R. Because by Thy holy Cross, Thou hast redeemed the world.

By assisting the poor, I can help and console Jesus in His suffering.
   Pray the Our Father, the Hail Mary, and the Glory Be.

Seventh Station:
Jesus falls the second time.

V. We adore Thee, O Christ, and we bless Thee,
R. Because by Thy holy Cross, Thou hast redeemed the world.

It is my repeated sins that caused Jesus to fall again.
    Pray the Our Father, the Hail Mary, and the Glory Be.

Eighth Station:
Jesus speaks to the daughters of Jerusalem.

V. We adore Thee, O Christ, and we bless Thee,
R. Because by Thy holy Cross, Thou hast redeemed the world.

May Jesus give me the grace to weep for my sins.
    Pray the Our Father, the Hail Mary, and the Glory Be.

Ninth Station:
Jesus falls the third time.

V. We adore Thee, O Christ, and we bless Thee,
R. Because by Thy holy Cross, Thou hast redeemed the world.

Give me the grace, O Lord, to correct my evil habits, which cause my many falls into sin.
    Pray the Our Father, the Hail Mary, and the Glory Be.

Tenth Station:
Jesus is stripped of His garments.

V. We adore Thee, O Christ, and we bless Thee,
R. Because by Thy holy Cross, Thou hast redeemed the world.

Strip me, O Lord, of attachment to the things of earth.
    Pray the Our Father, the Hail Mary, and the Glory Be.

Eleventh Station:
Jesus is nailed to the Cross.

V. We adore Thee, O Christ, and we bless Thee,
R. Because by Thy holy Cross, Thou hast redeemed the world.

May my heart be nailed to the Cross of Jesus so as never to be separated from His love.
Pray the Our Father, the Hail Mary, and the Glory Be.

Twelfth Station:
Jesus dies on the Cross.

V. We adore Thee, O Christ, and we bless Thee,
R. Because by Thy holy Cross, Thou hast redeemed the world.

Do I try to live for Jesus? He died for me.
Pray the Our Father, the Hail Mary, and the Glory Be.

Thirteenth Station:
Jesus is taken down from the Cross.

V. We adore Thee, O Christ, and we bless Thee,
R. Because by Thy holy Cross, Thou hast redeemed the world.

May the Mother of Christ intercede for us in the hour of death.
Pray the Our Father, the Hail Mary, and the Glory Be.

Fourteenth Station:
Jesus is placed in the sepulcher.

V. We adore Thee, O Christ, and we bless Thee,
R. Because by Thy holy Cross, Thou hast redeemed the world.

May I die to the world and to myself so that I may rise gloriously with Christ.
Pray the Our Father, the Hail Mary, and the Glory Be.

5

Thoughts for Meditation

(from *The Armor of God*)

Thoughts on Faith and Belief

"There is no God; the world is only a machine."
Did you ever know a machine without a designer?

Did you ever know a designer without intelligence?

Did you ever see a shadow that was not caused by light?

Have you ever read a book that was not first in the mind of the author?
Then you have seen a world without God!

Remember the words of the soldier at Bataan: "There are no atheists in foxholes."

⌒

"I am an atheist: I do not believe in God."
Would there ever be prohibition unless there was something to prohibit? Would there ever be anti-cigarette laws unless there were cigarettes? How could there be atheists unless there was something to believe in?

Atheism is not a doctrine; it is a cry of wrath.

"By night, an atheist half believes there is a God."

Before you deny God, ask yourself why you deny Him. Is it because of the way you live? A poem of Arthur Hugh Clough satirized those who wish there were no God because He interferes with their dishonesty, their lawlessness, or their license.

> There is no God, the wicked saith,
> And truly it's a blessing,
> For what He might have done with us
> It's better only guessing.
>
> There is no God, or if there is,
> The tradesman thinks, 'twere funny
> That He should take it ill in me
> To make a little money.
>
> There is no God, a youngster thinks,
> Or really, if there may be,
> He surely didn't mean a man
> Always to be a baby.
>
> Some others, also, to themselves,
> Who scarce so much as doubt it,
> Think there is none, when they are well,
> And do not think about it.

"Christ is a good man, a great humanitarian."
If Christ is not all He claimed to be, the Son of the living God, then He was not a good man! A good man never lies; but He was a liar if He was not God, for He said that He was God.

A good man never leads others into false belief. But He asked that men die for belief in His divinity, which they are doing even in this day.

If Christ was not God, then He not only was not a good man; He was the most villainous impostor and scoundrel the world has ever seen.

If Christ is not God, He is the antichrist.

❧

"I have no need of religion."
No man has need of religion who is self-righteous, who is all he wants to be, and all he ought to be. The man who never made a mistake has no need of an eraser; the man who never did anything wrong has no need of a Redeemer.

Our Lord Himself has said: "Those who are well have no need of a physician" (see Luke 5:31).

❧

"We have no freedom; our wills are determined."
Then why do we say "thanks" for a favor?

❧

"There is no right or wrong: it all depends on your point of view."
If there is no difference between right and wrong, how can people like Hitler be wrong, and how can we be right? Why have we ever been at war, if it is not because right is more precious than life?

❧

"It makes no difference what you believe; it all depends on how you act."
It makes no difference whether you have any rules in football; it all depends on how you play. It makes no difference whether you believe that triangles have three sides; it all depends on how you draw. Can we not see that if we believe wrongly, we will act wrongly?

The trouble with Hitler was that he practiced what he preached. Because his doctrine was wrong, his deeds were wrong. Because Nazism as a creed is wrong, its workings are wicked.

"Christianity has been tried and found wanting by the modern world."
Certainly, but did you ever know a Catholic who not only knew that he did wrong, but also wished that he had not? A Catholic who does wrong still believes his Faith is true.

There is always hope for the man who knows that he is doing wrong, but there is no hope for the man who, in doing wrong, calls the wrong right.

The Catholic gets off the road like anyone else, but he never throws away the map.

"Christianity has been found hard and not tried" (G. K. Chesterton).

Thoughts on the Spiritual Battle

The great assurance of victory is our correspondence with the Divine Will: "If God be for us, who is against us?" (Rom. 8:31).

⁊

Can our enemies' zeal for the cause of anti-God be overcome by our indifference to God?

⁊

God will not save our skin, but He will do everything to save our soul.

⁊

Death is not the greatest disaster in the world; sin is. "And fear ye not them that kill the body, and are not able to kill the soul: but rather fear him that can destroy both soul and body in hell" (Matt. 10:28).

⁊

The evil in the world must not make me doubt the existence of God. There could never be evil unless there was good.

God is not to be called "good" because He does our will, nor "evil" because He does not.

It is not easy to explain why God permits evil, but it is impossible for an atheist to explain the existence of goodness.

Why should a spiritless, soulless, crossless, Godless universe become the center of faith, purity, sacrifice, and martyrdom? How can decency be the decent thing, if there is no God?

Since God is love, why should we be surprised that want of it should end in pain, hate, broken hearts, and war?

There are only two philosophies of life: the Christian, which says: first the fast, then the feast; and the pagan, which says: first the feast, then the headache.

In either case, there is pain. The Christian never ends with it, even if he waits until the end of time.

There is a greater tragedy than death: the victory of evil.

We foolishly think sometimes that all God does is to see the evil we do! Do not be so discouraged. He sees every good act, every charity to our neighbor, every suppressed evil word, every drink of water given in His name.

God is not a tribal God; He is not the God of any one nation or people, but the God and Father of all, who made men of *one* blood to dwell upon the earth.

≈

"But if we all pray to God—the Germans, the Japanese, the English, the Americans, and so forth—on whose side is God?"

God's side is determined not by geography, but by those who do His will. If Germans, English, Japanese, and Americans prayed right, they would all be praying for the same intention: "*Thy will* be done on earth as it is in heaven."

And what is that will? The reign of justice and charity in the hearts of men.

≈

It was a soldier who first uttered the words recalled by the Church at Communion: "Lord, I am not worthy that thou shouldst enter under my roof: but only say the word, and my servant shall be healed" (see Matt. 8:8).

≈

The Breviary, which priests read daily, offers praise to Judas Maccabeus, who refused to surrender to superior enemy forces and died saying: "God forbid we should ... flee away from them [i.e., our enemies]; but if our time be come, let us die manfully for our brethren, and leave no cause to question our honor" (see 1 Macc. 9:10).

≈

Isaiah heard the seraphim around the throne of God address Him as the Lord of Armies. "Holy, holy, holy, the Lord God of hosts, all the earth is full of his glory" (Isa. 6:3).

≈

Life is a battle. St. Paul himself said: "I have fought the good fight, I have finished the race, I have kept the faith" (see 2 Tim. 4:7).

In a similar spirit, he enjoined Timothy: "This precept I commend to thee, O son Timothy; according to the prophecies going before on thee, that thou war in them a good warfare" (1 Tim. 1:18).

☙

"Share in suffering as a good soldier of Christ Jesus" (see 2 Tim. 2:3)

☙

The soldier's armor in the great battle of life is as follows: "Stand therefore, having your loins girt about with truth, and having on the breastplate of justice, and your feet shod with the preparation of the gospel of peace: in all things taking the shield of faith, wherewith you may be able to extinguish all the fiery darts of the most wicked one. And take unto you the helmet of salvation, and the sword of the Spirit (which is the word of God)" (Eph. 6:14–17).

☙

There is a war inside me: the flesh against the spirit. "I see another law in my members, fighting against the law of my mind, and captivating me in the law of sin, that is in my members" (Rom. 7:23).

☙

I am not fighting for a freedom that means the right to do whatever I *please* but for a freedom that means the right to do whatever I *ought*. Oughtness implies law; law implies intelligence, and intelligence implies God.

☙

I am not fighting merely to make the world safe for democracy; I am fighting to preserve the roots of democracy—the moral law rooted not in power, but in God.

☙

I am not fighting for freedom *from* something, but for freedom *for* something: the glorious freedom to call my soul my own and then to save it in cooperation with God's grace.

⁀

I must not be ashamed if I am fearful and if my whole being shrinks in dread, for the Lord in the garden before going to the battle of Calvary prayed: "If it be possible, let this chalice pass from me. Nevertheless not as I will, but as thou wilt" (Matt. 26:39).

What I must fear is my unwillingness to fulfill the will of God as revealed by the present circumstances of life. Not my will but thine be done (see Luke 22:42).

⁀

If a sparrow does not fall to the ground without God's knowing it, then a man does not fall. Nothing is beyond God's control. Even on the lake during the storm, the disciples, who all were experienced sailors, were reproved by Him for their lack of faith.

He did not mean that their fears were groundless, for many have been drowned at sea, but rather that they should have faced such a crisis with greater confidence and trust in Him.

⁀

Teach us, good Lord, to serve Thee as Thou deservest; to give and not to count the cost; to fight and not to heed the wounds; to toil and not to seek for rest; to labor and not to ask for any reward, save that of knowing that we do Thy will through Jesus Christ Our Lord. Amen. (St. Ignatius Loyola)

Thoughts on Prayer and Sacrifice

We do not pray in order that we may change God's will; we pray rather to change our own.

꩜

We do not pray that we may have good things; we pray rather that we may be good.

꩜

The perfect prayer is not one in which we tell God what we wish from Him, but rather one in which we ask God what He wishes from us.

꩜

Do not pray only in an emergency. The plea of strangers is never as effective as the plea of friends. Do not think of God only in times of distress or danger. Heaven is not a firehouse, and God does not put out all the fires.

꩜

Some men act toward God as they act toward their country. They seek to avoid paying taxes, to escape public burdens, but when their property rights are attacked, they call on their country most vociferously.

*

"Out of the abundance of the heart the mouth speaketh" (Matt. 12:34). The more we love our business, the more we talk about it; the more we love God, the more we pray.

*

Do not make all your prayers, prayers of petition. What would a young man think of a young lady who suffered from give-me-itis, who did nothing but ask favors?

Where there is love, we seek rather to give than to receive. Such is the test of a real love of God.

When God does answer your prayers of petition, do you ever thank Him for His gift?

> And it came to pass, as he was going to Jerusalem, He passed through the midst of Samaria and Galilee. And as He entered into a certain town, there met him ten men that were lepers, who stood afar off and lifted up their voice saying: "Jesus, Master, have mercy on us." Whom when he saw he said: "Go and show yourselves to the priests." And it came to pass as they went, they were made clean, and one of them, when he saw that he was made clean, went back, with a loud voice glorifying God. And he fell on his face before his feet, giving thanks, and this was a Samaritan, and Jesus answering, said: "Were not ten made clean? And where are the nine? There is no one found to return and give glory to God, but this stranger." And He said to him, "Arise, go thy way, for thy faith has made thee whole." (Luke 17:11–19)

*

You cannot always depend on prayers to be answered the way you want them answered, but you can always depend on God.

God, the loving Father, often denies us those things that in the end would prove harmful to us. Every boy wants a revolver at four, and no father yet has ever granted that request. Why should we think God is less wise? Someday we will thank God not only for what He gave us but also for that which He refused.

⁂

We should never pray for anything without at the same time submitting to God's will. Petition is inseparable from resignation, since God is good. When our will is one with God's will, then nothing can happen to us except what God wills; thus, we will never be disappointed.

As they say in Ireland when it rains and spoils a picnic: "Well, 'tis a good day to save your soul."

⁂

God will not supply every *want*, but He will supply every *need*. The trouble is that we want what we do not need.

⁂

Sometimes God answers prayers in a way different from what we ask. St. Monica had a son who was very immoral and proud. For years, she prayed to God for his conversion. Hearing that he planned on going to Italy, she renewed her prayers to God that he might be prevented from doing so, for she feared evil companionship there. But her son sailed despite her prayers.

While in Milan, he heard St. Ambrose preach and became a convert and one of the greatest bishops of the Church: St. Augustine. His mother's particular petition was denied, but her general petition was granted.

Commenting on it afterward, St. Augustine said: "O God, Thou in the depth of Thy counsels, hearing the main point of her desire, regarded not what she *then asked*, that Thou mightest make me what she ever *desired*."

Prayer is not the breaking down of the reluctance of God; it is rather the opening of a door. "Behold, I stand at the door and knock." The latch is on our side and not His. Prayer opens that door.

"Behold, I stand at the door and knock. If any man listens to my voice and opens the door to me, I will come into him and will sup with him, and he with me" (see Rev. 3:20).

The perfect prayer is one in which we seek to identify our will with God's will. "Thy will be done on earth as it is in Heaven" (Matt. 6:10).

When you pray, do not do all the talking! Listen! We are impolite when we pray, chattering, and mumbling all the time, but never giving God a chance to get a word in edgewise. "Speak Lord, for Thy servant heareth" (1 Kings [1 Sam.] 3:9).

If we keep pounding away with our hammers, how can the Divine Architect tell us how we ought to build?

If you are in the state of grace, God dwells in your heart. Hence, do not think of God being "way up there"; think of Him being on the inside.

Because our body is a temple, we should try to keep God dwelling therein. This is the basic reason for purity.

It is really not so important what we say to God; it is important what He says to us.

No one else in the world has a heart just like you, nor has he the same problems and worries and sins. That is why you should often make up your own prayers. Suppose you met our Divine Lord alone on the shores of Galilee. What would you say to Him? Say it now.

Prayer is not asking God to put Himself at our disposal.

> And James and John, the sons of Zebedee, came to him, saying: "Master we desire that whatsoever we shall ask, thou wouldst do it for us." But he said to them: "What would you that I should do for you?" And they said: "Grant to us that we may sit, one at thy right hand, and the other on thy left hand, in thy glory." And Jesus said to them: "You know not what you ask. Can you drink of the chalice that I drink of, or be baptized with the baptism wherewith I am baptized?" But they said to him: "We can." And Jesus said to them: "You shall indeed drink of the chalice that I drink of, and with the baptism wherewith I am baptized, you shall be baptized. But to sit on my right hand, or on my left hand, is not mine to give to you, but to them for whom it is prepared." (Mark 10:35–40)

Do not think that you have to be on your knees to pray. Sacred Scripture tells us: "Pray always." This means there is also the Prayer of Action.

Hence, never undertake any duty, whether it be typing a letter, dressing children, sitting down to a meal, going to a movie, listening to a dull story, studying, or digging, without doing it in the name of God. It then becomes a prayer.

Every action is an unsigned check; when we offer it in the name of God, we sign God's name to it and give it the value of a prayer.

A disappointment, a contradiction, a harsh word, an undeserved rebuke, a pain, a loss borne patiently in His name and endured as in His presence, is worth more than any prayer said by the lips.

The first thing in the morning, offer yourself to God, body and soul, reason and senses, purpose and desires, to be for that day whatever God wants you to be as revealed in the circumstances of life.

Say to God in some such language as this: "Thou knowest, good Lord, that I am tempted to get angry with, or to be jealous of (*mention the person or persons*), to take Thy Holy Name in vain, and (*mention the ways you are apt to sin or you have in the past*). But, dear Lord, for the love of Thee, I want to pass this day without committing these sins, or any other sins in thought, word, or deed. Please help me. Without You, I can do nothing; with You, I can do anything."

Our Divine Lord never preached on the dignity of labor. But He who carpentered the universe also worked at a carpenter's bench making wagon wheels, mending flat roofs, and fixing children's wagons. There is no work that cannot be made a prayer.

Our Lord never discoursed on equality: He spoke to the Samaritans, ate with publicans and sinners, and offered His life for all men.

In addition to the Prayer of Action, there is the Prayer of Sacrifice. The only way we can prove that we love anyone is by sacrifice.

Love does not mean to have, to own, to possess. It means to be had, to be owned, to be possessed. It is the giving of oneself for another. That is why we speak of "arrows and darts of love"—something that wounds.

And the day men forget that love is synonymous with sacrifice, they will ask what kind of a God is it who asks for mortification and self-denial. "Greater love than this no man hath, that he lay down his life for his friends" (John 15:13).

⁘

At least three times a day, deny yourself some tiny, lawful, legitimate pleasure, such as the extra cigarette, the second drink, or the extra lump of sugar, in order to discipline your spirit and keep mastery over yourself for the love of God.

These little "deaths" are so many rehearsals for the final death. Dying is a masterpiece, and to do it well, we must die daily: "If anyone wishes to come after me ... let him take up his *cross daily*" (Luke 9:23).

⁘

Mortification does not mean that we "give up" something; it means that we make an exchange. We do not "give up" our worldly pleasures; we exchange them for peace of soul.

Hence, those who speak of sacrifice as the negation of life seem never to understand that all love involves a choice: Adam chose between a fruit and a garden, as we have to choose between the world and Christ.

In our choice, we get something back in exchange: misery if we choose sin, peace if we choose Christ. "Or what exchange shall a man give for his soul?" (Matt. 16:26).

⁘

Make the sacrifice of not saying the nasty word or answering an insulting remark in kind. For in that way, we pull ourselves down to the vulgarity we condemn in others. No one will ever get ahead of us so long as he stays behind to kick us.

⌒

Catholics call the trials and disappointments of life "crosses." That means we consider them redemptive. "If anyone wishes to come after me, let him deny himself, and take up his cross daily and follow me" (Luke 9:23). Wherein do I take the cross daily?

⌒

Sacrifice without love is pain.
  Pain with love is sacrifice.
  Pain without love is misery.

⌒

Love without pain is heaven.
  Love with pain is purgatory.
  Pain without love is hell.

⌒

Pain in itself is not unbearable; it is the failure to understand its meaning that is unbearable. If pain and suffering had no reason, our Divine Lord would never have embraced it.

By patiently accepting each pain in union with His Cross, we become redeemers with a small r, as He is a Redeemer with a capital R.

⌒

Everyone who suffers is on a cross. Some ask to be taken down, like the thief on the left. Others want to be taken up, like the thief on the right.

⌒

Those who would rob divine justice of hell would rob the sovereignty of law of its prisons and the Christ of His Cross.

༄

"Bear one another's burdens," St. Paul tells us (Gal. 6:2). This is difficult to do unless we love God.

༄

Our Lord is walking through the world in disguise: as a soldier, as a tramp, as a neighbor, as a passerby, as a child, as a paralytic, as the blind, as the deaf. It is not for me to inquire whether they are worthy or not. That judgment belongs to God.

It is sufficient to know that they are creatures of God.

> "For I was hungry, and you gave me to eat; I was thirsty, and you gave me drink; I was a stranger, and you took me in; naked and you covered me; I was sick, and you visited me; I was in prison, and you came to me."
>
> Then the just will answer him, saying, "Lord, when did we see thee hungry, and feed thee; or thirsty, and give thee drink? And when did we see thee a stranger and take thee in; or naked, and clothe thee? Or when did we see thee sick, or in prison, and come to thee?"
>
> And the king answering shall say to them, "Amen, I say to you, as long as you did it for one of my least brethren, you did it for me." (Matt. 25:35–40)

༄

I shall make any sacrifices to which my country may call me—serve at the front, buy bonds, pay high taxes, labor long hours in factory or home, accept inconveniences—*in reparation for my sins.*

There is a thrill in paying off a debt, and we are all in debt to God! "Forgive us our trespasses"—that is, our debts.

The thief crucified on the right hand of Our Lord offered his cross in reparation for his sins: "And we indeed justly; for we are receiving the due reward of our deeds." In one day he blotted out his sins: "Amen, I say to thee, this day thou shalt be with me in paradise" (Luke 23:41, 43).

I will sacrifice and suffer gladly so that, through the example of my patience, others may come to know something of the blessedness of having found God. We live in a universe where the good or evil that one does has social repercussions.

A stone thrown into the ocean affects even the most distant shore.

Doctors graft skin from the body to the face when it is burned, and they transfuse blood from one member of society to another.

Now, if it is possible to graft skin, why is it not possible to graft prayer; if it is possible to transfuse blood, why is it not possible to transfuse sacrifice?

The sacrifices I make can therefore be applied to others: to a friend in battle; to a wife back home; to a brother who has been away from the sacraments for years; to a sister who has a bad marriage; to little children, that they may grow up as worthy children of God; and above all for the peace of the world.

Thoughts on Looking into My Soul

I may not believe in taxation, but taxation is inescapable. I may not believe that one day, God will judge me, but the judgment is inescapable. "It is appointed unto men once to die, and after this the judgment" (Heb. 9:27).

*

"For what doth it profit a man if he gain the whole world and suffers the loss of his own soul? Or what exchange shall a man give for his soul? For the Son of Man shall come in the glory of His Father with his angels: and then will he will render to every man according to his works" (Matt. 16:26–27).

*

"Then shall the King say to them that shall be on his right hand: 'Come, ye blessed of my Father, possess you the Kingdom prepared for you from the foundation of the world. For I was hungry, and you gave me to eat, I was thirsty, and you gave me to drink; I was a stranger, and you took me in; naked, and you covered me; sick, and you visited me; I was in prison, and you came to me.' Then shall the just answer him saying: 'Lord, when did we see thee hungry, and fed thee; thirsty, and gave thee drink? And when did we see thee a stranger, and took thee in, or naked, and covered thee? Or when did we see thee sick or in prison and came to thee?' And the King answering shall say to them: 'Amen I say to you, as long as you did it to one of these my least brethren, you did it to me.' Then he shall say to them also that shall be on his left hand: 'Depart from me, you cursed, into everlasting fire which was prepared for the devil and his angels. For I was hungry, and you gave me not to eat; I was thirsty, and you gave me not to drink. I was a stranger, and you took me not in; naked and you covered me not; sick and in prison, and you did not visit me.' Then they also shall answer him, saying: 'Lord, when did we see thee hungry, or thirsty, or a stranger, or naked, or sick, or in prison, and did not minister to thee?' Then he shall answer them, saying: 'Amen I say to you, as long as you did it not to one of these least, neither did you do it to me' (Matt. 25:34–45).

How Do I Stand in My Duties toward God?

"'Thou shalt love the Lord thy God with all thy whole heart, and with thy whole soul, and with thy whole mind.' This is the great and first commandment" (Matt. 22:37–38).

Do I seek to know Him, to love Him, and to serve Him? I know that I ought to do it, and I know I would like to do it, and I know I am not doing it, and I know I hate to be reminded about it.

How Do I Stand in My Duties toward My Neighbor?

"Thou shalt love thy neighbor as thyself " (Matt. 22:39).

⌒

My neighbor is often my enemy. "And as you would that men should do to you, do you also to them in like manner. And if you love them that love you, what thanks are to you? for sinners also love those that love them. . . . And if you lend to them of whom you hope to receive, what thanks are to you? for sinners also lend to sinners, for to receive as much. But love ye your enemies: do good, and lend, hoping for nothing thereby:

and your reward shall be great, and you shall be the sons of the Highest; for he is kind to the unthankful, and to the evil" (Luke 6:31–35).

☙

"If any man say, 'I love God,' and hateth his brother, he is a liar. For he that loveth not his brother, whom he seeth, how can he love God, whom he seeth not? And this commandment we have from God, that he who loveth God, love also his brother (1 John 4:20–21).

☙

Am I continually boasting and considering myself superior to my neighbor, either because he is ignorant, or poor, or a member of a certain class or race? "And whosoever shall exalt himself shall be humbled, and he that humbles himself shall be exalted" (Matt. 23:12).

"There is neither Jew nor Greek; there is neither slave nor free … for you are all one in Christ Jesus" (see Gal. 3:28).

How Do I Stand in Relation to Myself? What Kinds of Thoughts and Desires Possess My Soul?

Do I realize that if it is wrong to do a certain thing, then it is wrong to think about that thing? That the way to keep my actions clean is to keep my thoughts clean? That it is not when the act has been committed that the danger to the soul begins, but when the thought has been freely and favorably accepted by my will?

> Do you know that your bodies are members of Christ? Shall I then take the members of Christ and make them members of a harlot? By no means! Or do you not know that he who cleaves to a harlot, becomes one body with her? "For the two," it says, "shall be in one flesh." But he who cleaves to the Lord is one spirit with Him. Flee immorality.

Every sin that a man commits is outside the body, but the immoral man sins against his own body. Or do you not know that your members are the temple of the Holy Spirit, who is in you, whom you have from God and that you are not your own? For you are bought at a great price. Glorify and bear God in your body. (see 1 Cor. 6:15–20)

But I say to you that whosoever shall look at a woman to lust after her, hath already committed adultery with her in his heart. (Matt. 5:28)

But the things which proceed out of the mouth come forth from the heart, and these things defile a man. For from the heart come forth evil thoughts, murders, adulteries, fornications, thefts, false testimonies, blasphemies. (Matt. 15:18–19)

Then when concupiscence hath conceived, it bringeth forth sin, but sin, when it is completed, begetteth death. (James 1:15)

For we ourselves also were some time unwise, incredulous, erring, slaves to various passions and pleasures, living in malice and envy, hateful, and hating one another. But when the goodness and kindness of God our Savior appeared, not by the works of justice which we have done, but according to his mercy, he saved us, by the laver of regeneration, and renovation of the Holy Spirit. (Titus 3:3–5)

Meats for the belly and the belly for the meats, but God will destroy both it and them. But the body is not meant for immorality, but for the Lord, and the Lord for the body. (1 Cor. 6:13)

How Do I Stand before God in My Words?

Do I realize that a spoken word is like a shot fired and that it can never be taken back? Do I spread evil about others, whether it be true or false?

Do I set myself up as a judge of others' actions? Is my speech clean? Do I take the name of God in vain?

> O generation of vipers, how can you speak good things whereas you are evil? For out of the abundance of the heart, the mouth speaks. The good man out of a good treasure bringeth forth good things, and the evil man out of an evil treasure brings forth evil things.
>
> But I say unto you, that of every idle word that man shall speak, they shall render an account on the day of judgment. For by thy words thou shalt be justified, and by thy words, thou shalt be condemned. (Matt. 12:34–37)

> Thou shalt not take the name of the Lord thy God in vain; for the Lord will not hold him guiltless that shall take the name of the Lord his God in vain. (Exod. 20:7)

> All things are clean to the clean, but for the defiled and unbelieving nothing is clean; for both their mind and their conscience are defiled. (Titus 1:15)

> Blessed are the pure in heart, for they shall see God. (Matt. 5:8)

☞

"The general is sorry to be informed that the foolish and wicked practice of profane cursing and swearing, a vice heretofore little known in an American army, is growing into fashion. He hopes the officers will, by example as well as by influence, endeavor to check it, and that both they and the men will reflect that we can have little hope of the blessing of Heaven on our arms if we insult it by our impiety and folly. Added to this, it is a vice so mean and so low, without any temptation, that every man of sense and character detests and despises it." (General George Washington)

How Do I Stand before God in My Deeds?

Do I sin by omission? Do I fail to be charitable to those who need my help, to edify by good example, to pray, to diffuse God's truth, to prevent scandal?

What will it profit, my brethren, if a man says he hath faith but hath not works? Shall faith be able to save him?" (James 2:14)

What, shall your brethren go to the fight, and will you sit here? (Num. 32:6)

I would that thou wert cold or hot, but because thou art lukewarm, and neither cold nor hot, I begin to vomit thee out of my mouth. (Rev. 3:15–16)

What Sins Do I Commit?

Am I guilty of any of these sins that manifest that I live not by Christ, but by the flesh?

Now the works of the flesh are manifest, which are fornication, uncleanness, immodesty, luxury, idolatry, witchcrafts, enmities, contentions, emulations, wraths, quarrels, dissensions, sects, envies, murders, drunkenness, revelings, and such like. Of which I foretell you, as I have foretold to you, that they who do such things shall not obtain the kingdom of God. (Gal. 5:19–21)

Do I say, "I want to be good, dear Lord, a little later on, but not now"? "Watch ye, therefore, for you know not when the Lord of the house will cometh, at evening, or at midnight, or at cockcrow, or in the morning; lest coming on a sudden, he find you sleeping. I say to you, I say to all, 'Watch'" (Mark 13:35–37).

☞

"Lord Jesus, I believe, and by Thy grace will ever believe and hold, and I know that it is true and will be true to the end of the world, that nothing great is done without suffering, without humiliation, and that all things are possible by means of it.

"To possess Thee, O Lover of souls, is happiness and the only happiness of the immortal soul! To enjoy the sight of Thee is the only happiness of eternity.

"At present, I may amuse and sustain myself with the vanities of sense and time, but they will not last forever.

"We shall be stripped of them when we pass out of this world. All shadows will one day be gone. And what shall I do then? There will be nothing left to me but Almighty God.

"God and my soul will be the only two beings left in the whole world, as far as I am concerned. He will be all in all, whether I wish it or no. What a strait I shall then be in if I do not love Him!" (St. John Henry Newman)

⌒

"Earth must fade away from my eyes, and I must anticipate the great and solemn truth, which I shall not fully understand until I stand before God in judgment, that to me there are but two beings in the whole world, God and myself.

"The sympathy of others, the pleasant voice, the glad eye, the smiling countenance, the thrilling heart, which at present are my very life, all will be away from me when Christ comes in judgment. I shall have to think of myself.

"My eye shall see Him; my heart will be full of Him. He will speak to me, and I shall be rendering to Him my own account.

"By self-restraint, by abstinence, by prayer, by meditation, by recollection, by penance, I now anticipate in my measure that dreadful season.

"By thinking of it beforehand, I hope to mitigate its terrors when it comes. By humbling myself now, I hope to escape humiliation then. By owning my faults now, I hope to avert the disclosures of that day. By judging myself now, I hope to be spared that judgment that mercy tempers not.

"I prepare now to meet my God; I retire, as it were, to my sick room and put my house in order.... I leave the goods of earth before they leave me." (St. John Henry Newman)

☞

"Did God send us, above all other men, into the world to be idle in spiritual matters? Is it our mission only to find pleasure in this world, in which we are merely pilgrims and sojourners? Are we more than sons of Adam, who, by the sweat of their brow, are to eat bread till they return to the earth out of which they are taken?

"Unless we have some work in hand, unless we are struggling, unless we are fighting with ourselves, we are not followers of those who 'through many tribulations entered into the kingdom of God.'

"A fight is the very token of a Christian. He is a soldier of Christ; high or low, he is this and nothing else.

"If we have triumphed over all mortal sin, then we must attack our venial sins; there is no help for it; there is nothing else to do if we would be soldiers of Jesus Christ.

"Everyone is made for his day; he does his work in his day; what he does is not the work of any other day, but of his own day; his work is necessary in order to prepare the work of that next day, which is not his, as a stepping-stone on which we, who come next, are to raise our own work." (St. John Henry Newman)

Thoughts on Encouragement

When you begin to be infinitely wicked, and God ceases to be infinitely merciful, then you can begin to despair.

⁓

We are not most wicked when we are most conscious of our sins, but when we are not conscious of them. When we realize we are sinners, we see by a better light. When we realize we are sick, we perceive the need of the Great Physician.

⁓

There is only one thing in the world worse than sin, and that is the refusal to recognize that we are sinners.

⁓

If I had never sinned, I never could call Christ "Savior."

⁓

Did not Our Lord say He would never reject any man coming to Him? "Him that cometh to me, I will not cast out" (John 6:37).

⌒

The thief on the cross died a thief, for he stole paradise! Paradise may be stolen again.

⌒

God loves you more than you love yourself. As St. Augustine said: "God loves us, everyone, as though there was but one of us to love."

⌒

Could an architect plan a building without planning its smallest details? Could God make a universe without a providential plan for every one of us?

"I am the good shepherd, and I know mine and mine know me, as the Father knoweth me, and I know the Father, and I lay down my life for my sheep. And other sheep I have that are not of this fold. Them also I must bring, and they shall hear my voice, and there shall be one fold and one shepherd" (John 10:14–16).

⌒

"What think you? If a man have a hundred sheep, and one of them should go astray, doth he leave not the ninety-nine in the mountains and go to seek that which is gone astray? And if it be so that he finds it, amen I say to you, he rejoices more for that than over the ninety-nine that went not astray. . . .

"Even so, it is not the will of your Father in Heaven that a single one of these little ones should perish" (Matt. 18:12–14).

⌒

"And he said; A certain man had two sons: and the younger of them said to his father: 'Father, give me the portion of substance that falleth to me.' And he divided unto them his substance, and not many days after, the younger son, gathering all together, went abroad into a far country; and there wasted his substance living riotously, and after he had spent all, there came a mighty famine in that country; and he began to be in want, and he went and cleaved to one of the citizens of that country. And he sent him into his farm to feed swine. And he would gladly have filled his belly with the husks the swine did eat, and no man gave unto him. And he returning to himself, he said: 'How many hired servants in my father's house abound with bread, and I here perish with hunger? I will arise, and I will go to my father, and say to him: "Father, I have sinned against heaven and before thee: I am not worthy to be called thy son. Make me as one of thy hired servants."' And rising up, he came to his father. And when he was yet a great way off, his father saw him, and he was moved with compassion, and running to him, he fell upon his neck and kissed him. And the son said to him: 'Father, I have sinned against heaven, and before thee. I am not worthy to be called thy son.' And the father said to his servants: 'Bring forth quickly the first robe, and put it on him, and put a ring on his hand, and shoes on his feet: and bring hither the fatted calf, and kill it, and let us eat and make merry'" (Luke 15:11–23).

◌

"And then come, and accuse me, saith the Lord: if your sins be as scarlet, they shall be made as white as snow: and if they are red as crimson, they shall be white as wool" (Isa. 1:18).

◌

A woman once went to the Curé of Ars, St. John Vianney, and said: "My husband has just fallen off a bridge — he has not been to the sacraments in twenty years. A double death! His soul is lost." Father Vianney answered: "Madam, there is a little distance between the bridge and the water" — enough time to make an act of contrition.

Never give up hope: "Him who cometh to me, I will not cast out" (John 6:37).

It is so hard to admit that one is a sinner; it is so hard to climb the hill of Calvary and kneel beneath a cross and ask for pardon and forgiveness. Certainly, it is hard. But it is harder to hang there.

Why do we feel so disgusted after we have sinned? For the same reason that we feel pain when we break a bone. Things are not as they *ought* to be; we have disturbed God's order. Remorse is the voice of God, calling us back again to peace.

The floating bell buoys on the ocean need no hands to ring them; the restless waves do the work. So does remorse toll the bells of an uneasy conscience.

The pleasures of the world are always delightful in anticipation, disgusting in retrospect. The joys of the spirit seem difficult in prospect but are thrilling in their possession. God is reminding us that our peace is in Him.

What death is in the physical order, sin is in the spiritual order: the loss of life. "The wages of sin is death" (Rom. 6:23). In one instance, we lose our physical life; in the other, our eternal life. And the loss of that kind of life is hell. "You have the name of being alive, and you are dead" (see Rev. 3:1).

Do not think of God as always looking around corners with an angel as a secretary to jot down all your sins. He is also looking at your good deeds, seeing every drink of cold water you give in His name, every visit to the sick you make in His name, every act of kindness you do for your fellow man in His name.

It is hard to understand why God should care so much for sinners; but does not a mother rejoice more at the recovery of her sick child than at the continued health of the rest of the family? Did not the Prodigal Son get the fatted calf, while the one who stayed at home was not so much as given a goat?

⤳

There are only two classes of people in the world: those who fall and stay down, and those who fall and get up again.

⤳

Count your resurrections as well as your falls.

Thoughts on the Eucharist

There are certain things in life too beautiful to be forgotten. That is why we revere the sacrifice of our soldiers on Memorial Day. The most beautiful thing about the life of Our Lord was His death. Everyone else came into the world to *live*; He came into it to *die*, "to give His life as a ransom for many" (Matt. 20:28).

His death was the *one thing* He wished to have remembered. He did not ask that men should write down His words in books. He did not ask that His deeds be recorded in history. But He did ask that men remember His death.

And in order that its memory might not be any haphazard narrative on the part of men, He Himself instituted the precise way it should be recalled.

⌒

The memorial was instituted the night before He died, at what has since been called the Last Supper. Taking bread into His hands, He said: "This is my Body, which shall be delivered for you"; that is, delivered unto death. Then, over the chalice of wine, He said, "This is my blood of the new covenant, which shall be shed for many unto remission of sins."

Thus, in an unbloody symbol of the parting of His blood from His body, by the separate consecration of bread and wine, Christ pledged Himself to death in the sight of God and men and represented His death, which was to come the next afternoon at three.

He was offering Himself as a victim to be immolated and that men might never forget that "greater love than this no one has, that one lay down his life for his friends" (John 15:13).

In order that this sacrifice would never be forgotten, He gave the divine command to the Church: "Do this in remembrance of me" (see Luke 22:19).

The Mass is the perpetuation of the Sacrifice of Calvary with the same Priest and the same Victim. The difference is that Calvary was a bloody sacrifice; the Mass is offered in an unbloody manner. Furthermore, on the Cross, Our Lord was alone; in the Mass, we are with Him.

We offer ourselves in the Mass with Christ through bread and wine. In the early Church, we would have brought these elements. Today we bring that which buys bread and wine. Hence the offertory collection.

We bring bread and wine because of all things in nature these two best represent the substance of life. Wheat is, as it were, the very marrow of the ground, and the grapes are its very blood; both give us the body and blood of life.

In bringing those two things, which give us life and nourish us, we are equivalently bringing ourselves to the Sacrifice of the Mass.

☞

We are therefore present at each and every Mass under the appearance of bread and wine, which stand as symbols of our body and blood. We are not passive spectators, as we might be while watching a spectacle in a theater, but we are co-offering our Mass with Christ.

We are on the altar symbolically under the appearance of bread and wine. But bread comes from wheat and wine from grapes, and neither becomes what they are, except by passing through, in one instance a mill, and in the other, a wine press.

Hence both are symbols of Christians who are called to suffer with Christ, that they may reign with Christ.

As the Consecration arrives, the priest, in obedience to the words of Our Lord, "Do this for a commemoration of me," takes bread in his hands and says: "This is the chalice of my Blood of the new and eternal testament." He does not consecrate the bread and wine together, but separately.

The separate consecration of the bread and wine is a symbolic representation of the separation of body and blood, and since the Crucifixion entailed that very mystery, Calvary is thus renewed on our altar. But Christ, as has been said, is not alone on our altar; we are with Him.

Hence, the words of consecration have a double sense; their primary signification is: "This is the Body of Christ; this is the Blood of Christ"; but their secondary signification is: "This is my body; this is my blood."

Some such sentiment as the following we should have in our heart at the moment of consecration: "I give myself to God. Here is my body. Take it. Here is my blood. Take it. Here is my soul, my will, my energy, my strength, my property, and my wealth—all that I have. It is Thine. Take it! Consecrate it! Offer it!

Offer it with thyself to the heavenly Father in order that He, looking down on this great sacrifice, may see only Thee, His Beloved Son, in whom He is well pleased.

"Transmute the poor bread of my life into Thy divine life; thrill the wine of my wasted life into Thy divine Spirit; unite my broken heart with Thy Heart; change my cross into a crucifix. Let not my abandonment and my sorrow and my bereavement go to waste.

Gather up the fragments, and as the drop of water is absorbed in wine, let my little cross be entwined with Thy great Cross so that I may purchase the joys of everlasting happiness in union with Thee.

"Consecrate these trials of my life, which would go unrewarded unless united with Thee; 'transubstantiate' me so that, like bread that is now Thy Body, and wine that is now Thy Blood, I, too, may be wholly Thine.

"I care not if the species remain, or that, like the bread and the wine, I seem to all earthly eyes the same as before.

"My station in life, my routine duties, my work, my family—all these are but the species of my life, which may remain unchanged; but the substance of my life, my soul, my mind, my will, my heart 'transubstantiate,' transform them wholly into Thy service, so that through me all may know how sweet is the love of Christ. Amen."

⸎

In the Offertory, we offered ourselves to God through Christ. In the Consecration, God accepted our offering in Christ, and He changes us into Christ. Now in the Communion, Christ gives Himself back to us.

⸎

We believe that Jesus Christ is really, truly, and substantially present in His Body and Blood, Soul and Divinity, on our altars under the appearance of bread. How do we know it? Our Lord told us, "This is my Body."

No one ever doubted these words of Our Lord until the year 1088, and then it was later retracted. The next denial came four centuries later. It is therefore relatively late in Christian history that mankind has been bold enough to say that Our Lord did not mean what He said about the Eucharist, or hell, or divorce.

If Christianity just meant a memory of Christ, how unsatisfying it would be! If Christ means no more to our lives than the example of His life twenty centuries ago, then it is difficult to see how He was God, and how He differed from man.

If He had no power to extend His life, His influence, His grace, His very Body and Blood through time to its very end, then He is under the same limitations of every man.

Life demands more than a souvenir to sustain it, and if Christ is the very life of Christians, He must be more than a memory.

It would not be enough to tell the animal: "See the way the plant lives; let that be your example." If Christ is to be our food and our life, it is fitting that He be with us, for it is of the nature of life to be localized and definite.

The plant life that is the food of the animal does not dwell on some distant planet, and neither does Christ, who is the food of the soul, dwell apart from us like an absentee landlord. He is with us; He is here, He has a dwelling.

The tabernacle is now de facto the localization of life, and it is there and only there that the downcast eyes of sin find wealth of purging tears; only there that the longings of hope are uplifted to look beyond the veil; only there that the scourged heart that bleeds, and bleeds afresh, at last breaks its silence in answer to the invitation: "Child, give me thy heart."

⤳

You would never pass by a friend without greeting him. Never pass by Our Lord in the Eucharist without a prayer. You and I have an opportunity to know the Judge before the day of our trial, and that friendship may avail us much in the hour of judgment.

Meditation before Communion
(Thomas à Kempis, *The Imitation of Christ*, book 4, chapter 12)

I am the Lover of purity and the Giver of all holiness. I seek a pure heart, and there is the place of my rest. Make ready for me a large dining room furnished and ready; there prepare ye for us (see Mark 14:15).

If you will have me come to you, and remain with you, purge out the old leaven, and make clean the habitation of your heart:

Shut out the whole world, and all the tumult of vices; sit like a sparrow solitary on the housetop, and think of your excesses in the bitterness of your soul.

For every lover prepares the best and fairest room for his dearly beloved, and hereby is known the affection of him who entertains his beloved.

Know, nevertheless, that you cannot sufficiently prepare yourself by the merit of any action of yours, even if you should prepare yourself a whole year together, and think of nothing else.

But it is out of my mere goodness and grace that you are suffered to come to my table; as if a beggar were invited to dinner by a rich man and had nothing else to return him for his benefits but to humble himself and give him thanks.

Do what you can, and do it diligently; not out of custom, or for necessity, but with fear, and reverence, and affection, receive the Body of thy beloved Lord your God, who vouchsafes to come to you.

I am He who has invited you: "I have commanded it to be done; I will supply what is wanting in you; come and receive me. You come that you may be sanctified by me and united to me; so that you may receive new grace and be inflamed anew to amendment. Neglect not this grace, but prepare thy heart with all diligence, and bring your beloved into your heart."

Prayer before Communion by St. Thomas Aquinas

O almighty, everlasting God, behold I draw near to the sacrament of Thy only-begotten Son, Our Lord Jesus Christ. I draw near, as a sick man to the Physician of life, as one defiled to the Fountain of mercy, as one blind to the Light of the eternal splendor, as one poor and needy to the Lord of heaven and earth. Wherefore, I implore the fullness of Thy infinite bounty that Thou wouldst vouchsafe to heal all my sickness, to wash away my defilement, to give light to my blindness, to enrich my poverty and clothe my nakedness, so that I may receive the Bread of Angels, the King of Kings and Lord of Lords, with such contrition and devotion, such purity and faith, such purpose and intention, as may avail to the welfare and salvation of my soul.

Grant me, I beseech Thee, to receive not only the sacrament of the Body and Blood of my Lord but also the very reality and efficacy of the sacrament. O most gracious God, grant me so to receive the Body of Thy only-begotten Son, Our Lord

Jesus Christ, that very Body that He took of the Virgin Mary, that I may be truly incorporated into His Mystical Body and so numbered among its members. O most loving Father, grant me, at last, to behold with open face, and forevermore, Thy beloved Son, whom I purpose to receive now in my pilgrimage, beneath the veils of this sacrament; who lives and reigns, God through everlasting ages. Amen.

Meditation after Communion
(Thomas à Kempis, *The Imitation of Christ*, book 4, chapter 12)

But not only should you prepare yourself by devotion before Communion, but you should also carefully keep yourself therein after receiving the sacrament; neither is the carefully guarding of yourself afterward less required than the devoutly preparing yourself before, for a good guard afterward is the best preparation for again obtaining greater grace.

For what renders a man very much indisposed is if he presently turns himself to seek exterior comforts.

Beware of much talk, remain in secret, and enjoy your God, for you have Him, whom all the world cannot take from you.

I am the one to whom you must wholly surrender yourself, so that from now on, you may lose all your care and live not in yourself, but in me.

Prayer after Communion by St. Thomas Aquinas

I humbly adore Thee, O God. I extol Thee, immortal King of angels. Thou art the perfect image of Thy eternal Father's substance! Thou art the splendor of His glory! Thou art His powerful word, supporting all things; Thee He hath seated at His right hand. Thy throne, O God, is forever and ever; a scepter of justice is the scepter of Thy reign. I bow before Thy sacred majesty; I acknowledge with the sincerest gratitude that Thou art my Redeemer, my Creator, and the supreme Arbiter of my eternal destiny. I desire to humble myself as profoundly for Thy sake as Thou art humbled for my love in the center of my soul and to consecrate to the glory of Thy name the whole extent of my being.

I give Thee thanks, eternal Father! For having, out of Thy pure mercy, without any deserts of mine, been pleased to feed my soul with the Body and Blood of Thy only Son, Our Lord Jesus Christ. I beseech Thee that this Holy Communion may not be to my condemnation but may prove an effectual remission of all my sins. May it strengthen my faith; encourage me in all that is good; deliver me from my vicious customs; remove all concupiscence; perfect me in charity, patience, humility, obedience, and in all other virtues. May it secure me against all the snares of my enemies, both visible and invisible; perfectly moderate all my inclinations, closely unite me to Thee, the true and only good, and happily settle me in unchangeable bliss. I now make it my hearty request that Thou wilt one day admit me, though an unworthy sinner, to be a guest at that divine banquet where Thou, with Thy Son and the Holy Ghost, art the true light, eternal fullness, everlasting joy, and perfect happiness of all the saints, through the same Jesus Christ Our Lord. Amen.

Benediction of the Blessed Sacrament

The purpose of Benediction is to express faith in the Real Presence of Christ in the Holy Eucharist, to adore His majesty, to obtain His blessing, to make reparation for outrages and insults offered to God, and to return Him thanks for His many benefits.

Hymns to the Blessed Sacrament

After the Blessed Sacrament has been placed on the altar, the following two hymns of veneration are sung:

O Salutaris Hostia

O Salutaris Hostia,
Quae caeli pandas ostium:
Bella premunt hostilia:
Da robur, fer auxilium.
Uni trinoque Domino
Sit sempiterna Gloria,
Qui vitam sine termino
Nobis donet in patria.

Tantum Ergo

Tantum ergo Sacramentum,
Veneremur cernui;
Et antiquum documentum
Novo cedat ritui;
Praestet fides supplementum
Sensuum defectui.
Genitori, Genitoque,
Laus et jubilatio;
Salus, honor, virtus quoque
Sit et benedictio;
Procedenti ab utroque
Compar sit laudatio.
Amen.

O Saving Victim

O saving Victim, opening wide
The gate of Heaven to man below!
Our foes press on from every side;
Thine aid supply, Thy strength bestow.
To Thy great Name be endless praise,
Immortal Godhead! One in Three!
O grant us endless length of days
In our true native land with Thee!

Down in Adoration Falling

Down in adoration falling,
Lo! The sacred Host we hail!
Lo! O'er ancient forms departing,
Newer rites of grace prevail;
Faith for all defects supplying
Where the feeble senses fail.
To the everlasting Father,
And the Son who reigns on high,
With the Holy Spirit proceeding,
Forth from each eternally,
Be salvation, honor, blessing,
Might, and endless majesty.
Amen.

LORD, TEACH US TO PRAY

The Divine Praises

Blessed be God.
Blessed be His holy Name.
Blessed be Jesus Christ, true God and true man,
Blessed be the Name of Jesus.
Blessed be His most Sacred Heart.
Blessed be His most Precious Blood.
Blessed be Jesus in the Most Holy Sacrament of the Altar.
Blessed be the great Mother of God, Mary most holy.
Blessed be her holy and immaculate conception.
Blessed be her glorious Assumption.
Blessed be the name of Mary, Virgin and Mother.
Blessed be St. Joseph, her most chaste spouse.
Blessed be God in His angels and in His saints.

Hymn of Praise

Holy God, we praise Thy Name!
Lord of all, we bow before Thee!
All on earth Thy scepter claim,
All in heaven above adore Thee:
Infinite Thy vast domain,
Everlasting is Thy reign.
Infinite Thy vast domain,
Everlasting is Thy reign.
Hark! The loud celestial hymn
Angel choirs above are raising:
Cherubim and Seraphim,
In unceasing chorus praising,
Fill the heavens with sweet accord:
Holy, Holy, Holy Lord!
Fill the heavens with sweet accord:
Holy, Holy, Holy Lord!

Holy Father, Holy Son,
Holy Spirit, Three we name Thee,
While in essence only One,
Undivided God we claim Thee:
And adoring bend the knee,
While we own the mystery.
And adoring bend the knee,
While we own the mystery.

Thoughts on the Blessed Mother

What would you think of one who professed to be a true friend of yours and yet never spoke to your mother? That is what Our Lord thinks of those who have no veneration to His Virgin Mother.

＝

If you could have preexisted your mother, would you not have made her the most beautiful woman and the best in the world? Well, Our Lord preexisted His Mother. We may, therefore, presume that He did that very thing.

＝

It is a Christian tradition that no one who is devoted to Our Lord's Mother is ever lost. There is a story to the effect that one day, as Our Lord was walking through the courts of heaven, He saw some souls who seemed to have won heaven quite easily. "Peter," he asked, "how did these souls gain entry into my kingdom?" Peter answered: "Don't blame me, Lord; every time I close a door, Your Mother opens a window."

＝

There were three forces contributing to the Fall of the human race: a disobedient man: Adam; a proud woman: Eve; and a tree. These three conspired for our Redemption. For the disobedient Adam, there was the obedient new Adam, Christ; for the proud woman Eve, there was the humble Virgin, Mary; and for the tree, the Cross.

Eve was given to Adam as a helpmate and failed him beneath the tree. Mary, giving birth to God Incarnate, ministered to Him in infancy, followed Him to Calvary, and stood by the tree of the Cross as the help-mate who failed not.

◠

Mary stood at the deathbed of the Cross. We pray in the Hail Mary: "Holy Mary, Mother of God, pray for us sinners, now and at the hour of our death. Amen." To whom could we better appeal for the grace of a happy death than to her who comforted her Son in His last moments on the Cross?

◠

Our Blessed Mother alone knows how to console those mothers whose sons are in battle, for her only Son died in the War of Calvary. As she looked up into the night sky and saw a golden star, she became the first Gold Star Mother of Christian times.

◠

If we could ever find anything we loved more than the flesh, the demands of the flesh would be less imperative. This is the "escape" a mother offers her boy when she says: "Don't do anything of which your mother would ever be ashamed." If there is that higher love of his mother, the boy will always have a consecrated sense of affection, something for which he will be willing to make sacrifices.

When a mother makes such an appeal to her son, she is merely echoing the lesson of the Savior, who, in giving His Mother to us as our Mother, equivalently said: "My children, never do anything of which your Mother would be ashamed."

Let a soul but love that Mother, and he will love her Divine Son, Jesus, who, in order to make satisfaction for the unlawful pleasure of the flesh, surrendered to us His last lawful attachment — His Mother.

⌒

The reason there is a degeneration in the moral order and a decay of decency is that men and women have lost the higher love. Ignoring Christ their Savior, who loved them unto death on Calvary, and Mary, who loved them unto becoming the Queen of Martyrs beneath that Cross, they have nothing for which to make the sacrifice.

⌒

Mary, who is the Virgin Most Pure, is also the Refuge of Sinners. She knows what sin is, not by the experience of its fall, not by tasting its bitter regrets, but by seeing what it did to her Divine Son.

⌒

Mary's purity is not a holier-than-thou purity, a standoffish holiness that gathers up its robes lest they be stained by the sinful; nor is it a despising purity that looks down upon the impure. Rather, it is a radiating purity that is no more spoiled by solicitude for the fallen than sunshine is sullied by a dirty windowpane through which it pours.

⌒

Mary was destined to have other children than Jesus, but they were to be born not of her flesh but of her heart. Mother of Christ was she at the Cross. Her firstborn in Bethlehem was brought forth in joy, but the curse of Eve hung about her labors at the Cross, for she was now, like Eve, bringing forth her children in sorrow.

At that moment Mary suffered the pangs of spiritual childbirth for the millions of souls who would ever be called to adoptive sonship of the Father, to brotherhood of Christ, and to the joy of calling her Mother.

The Angelus

The angel of the Lord declared unto Mary.
And she conceived by the Holy Spirit.

Hail Mary, full of grace, the Lord is with thee; blessed art thou among women and blessed is the fruit of thy womb, Jesus. Holy Mary, Mother of God, pray for us sinners, now and at the hour of our death. Amen.

Behold the handmaid of the Lord.
Be it done unto me according to thy word.

Hail Mary ...

And the Word was made flesh.
And dwelt among us.

Hail Mary ...

Pray for us, O holy Mother of God.
That we may be made worthy of the promises of Christ.

Let us pray. Pour forth, we beseech Thee, O Lord, Thy grace into our hearts, that we to whom the Incarnation of Christ, Thy Son, was made known by the message of an angel, may by His Passion and Cross be brought to the glory of His Resurrection, through the same Christ Our Lord. Amen.

Christ, hast vouchsafed to make glad the whole world. Grant, we beseech Thee, that, through the intercession of the Virgin Mary, His Mother, we may attain the joys of eternal life, through the same Christ Our Lord. Amen.

Regina Coeli

V. Queen of Heaven, rejoice, Alleluia.
R. For He whom thou didst deserve to bear, Alleluia.

V. Hath risen as He said, Alleluia.
R. Pray for us to God, Alleluia.

V. Rejoice and be glad, O Virgin Mary! Alleluia.
R. Because Our Lord is truly risen, Alleluia.

Let us pray. O God, who by the Resurrection of Thy Son, Our Lord Jesus Christ, hast vouchsafed to make glad the whole world, grant, we beseech Thee, that, through the intercession of the Virgin Mary, His Mother, we may attain the joys of eternal life.
Through the same Christ Our Lord. Amen.

Prayer to Our Lady of Perpetual Help

Behold at thy feet, O Mother of Perpetual Help, a wretched sinner who has recourse to thee, and confides in thee.

O Mother of mercy, have pity on me. I hear thee called by all the refuge and the hope of sinners: be then my refuge and my hope.

Assist me, for the love of Jesus Christ; stretch forth thy hand to a miserable fallen creature who recommends himself to thee and who devotes himself to thy service forever.

I bless and thank Almighty God, who, in His mercy, has given me this confidence in thee, which I hold to be a pledge of my eternal salvation.

It is true that in the past, I have miserably fallen into sin because I had no recourse to thee. I know that now, with thy help, I shall conquer.

I know, too, that thou wilt assist me if I recommend myself to thee; but I fear that in time of danger, I may neglect to call on thee and thus lose my soul.

This grace, then, I ask of thee, and I beg, with all the fervor of my soul, that, in all the attacks of Hell, I may ever have recourse to thee.

O Mary, help me. O Mother of Perpetual Help, never suffer me to lose my God.

The Memorare

Remember, O most gracious Virgin Mary, that never was it known that anyone who fled to thy protection, implored thy help, or sought thy intercession was left unaided. Inspired with this confidence, I fly unto thee, O Virgin of virgins, my mother; to thee I come, before thee I stand, sinful and sorrowful. O Mother of the Word Incarnate, despise not my petitions; but in thy mercy hear and answer me. Amen.

Hail, Holy Queen

Hail Holy Queen, Mother of Mercy. Hail our life, our sweetness, and our hope! To thee do we cry, poor banished children of Eve; to thee do we send up our sighs, mourning, and weeping in this vale of tears.

Turn, then, most gracious advocate, thine eyes of mercy toward us; and after this our exile, show unto us the blessed fruit of thy womb, Jesus.

O clement, O loving, O sweet Virgin Mary.

Pray for us, O holy Mother of God.

That we may be made worthy of the promises of Christ. Amen.

6

Prayers of Meditation and Petition

(from *The Armor of God* and *Holy Hour* booklets)

Christ to a Faithful Soul

(Thomas à Kempis, *The Imitation of Christ*, book 3, chapter 1)

Happy are the souls that hear the Lord speaking within them, and from their mouths receive the word of comfort.

Happy are the ears that hear the accents of the divine whisper and take no notice of the whisperings of the world.

Happy ears, indeed, are those ears that hearken to truth itself teaching within, and who hearken not to the voice that sounds without.

Happy eyes that are shut to outward things and attentive to the interior. Happy they who penetrate into internal things and endeavor to prepare themselves more and more by daily exercises, the attaining to heavenly secrets.

Happy are they who seek to be wholly intent on God and who rid themselves of every worldly impediment.

Mind these things, O my soul, and shut the doors of your senses, that you may hear what the Lord your God speaks within you.

Thus says your Beloved: I am your salvation, your peace, and your life; abide in me, and you shall find peace.

Leave alone all transitory things, and seek things eternal.

What are all temporal things, but deceit? And what will all things created avail you, if you be forsaken by your Creator?

Cast off, then, all earthly things; make yourself agreeable to your Creator and faithful to Him so that you may attain to true happiness.

Prayer to Follow the Example of Jesus Christ
(Thomas à Kempis, *The Imitation of Christ*, book 3, chapter 18)

My Child, I came down from heaven for your salvation; I took upon me your miseries, not of necessity, but moved out of love, that you might learn patience, and might bear, without repining, the miseries of this life. For, from the hour of my birth till my expiring on the Cross, I was never without suffering.

Lord, because You were patient in life, especially in fulfilling the commandment of the Father, it is fitting that I, a wretched sinner, should, according to Your will, take all with patience and, as long as You wish, support the burden of this corruptible life, in order to gain my salvation.

Oh, what great thanks am I obliged to return to You for having vouchsafed to show me and all the faithful a right and good way to an everlasting kingdom.

Had You not gone before and instructed us, who would have cared to follow?

Behold, we are still tepid, notwithstanding all the miracles and instructions we have heard. What, then, would it be, if we had not this great light whereby to follow You?

Prayer against Evil Thoughts
(Thomas à Kempis, *The Imitation of Christ*, book 3, chapter 23)

O Lord, my God, be not far from me. O my God, hasten to help me, for diverse evil thoughts and great fears have risen up against me, afflicting my soul. How shall I pass them without hurt? How shall I break through them?

"And the people shall take them, and bring them into their place: and the house of Israel shall possess them in the land of the Lord for servants and handmaids: and they shall make them captives that had taken them, and shall subdue their oppressors" (Isa. 14:2).

I, saith He, will go before thee, and will humble the great ones of the earth. I will open the gates of the prison and reveal to thee hidden secrets.

Do, as you say, Lord, and let all these wicked thoughts flee from Your face.

This is my hope and my only comfort, to fly to You in all tribulations, to confide in You, to call on You from my heart, and patiently to look for Your consolation.

Prayer for the Enlightening of the Mind
(Thomas à Kempis, *The Imitation of Christ*, book 3, chapter 23)

Enlighten me, O good Jesus, with the brightness of internal light, and cast all darkness from the dwelling of my heart. Restrain my many wandering thoughts, and suppress all of the temptations that violently assault me.

Fight strongly for me, and overcome these wicked beasts—I mean these alluring concupiscences—that peace may be made in Your power, and the abundance of Your praise may resound in Your holy court, which is a clean conscience.

Command the winds and storms; say to the sea, "Be still" and to the north wind, "Blow thou not"; and a great calm shall ensue.

Send forth Your light and Your truth to shine upon the earth; for I am as the earth, empty and void until You illumine me.

Pour out Your grace from above; water my heart with the dew of heaven. Send down the waters of devotion to wash the face of the earth, to bring forth good and perfect fruit.

Lift up my mind, oppressed with the load of sins, and raise my whole desire toward heavenly things, that, having tasted the sweetness of the happiness above, I may have no pleasure in thinking of the things of the earth.

Draw me away, and deliver me from all unstable comfort of creatures; for no created thing can fully quiet and satisfy my desires.

Join me to Yourself by an inseparable bond of love, because You alone can satisfy the lover, and without You, all things are frivolous.

Prayer for Charity and Tolerance
(attributed to Eusebius, bishop of Caesarea)

May I be no man's enemy, and may I be the friend of that which is eternal and abides. May I never quarrel with those nearest me; and if I do, may I be reconciled quickly. May I never devise evil against any man; if any devise evil against me, may I escape uninjured and without the need of hurting him.

May I love, seek, and attain only that which is good. May I wish for all men's happiness and envy none. May I never rejoice in the ill fortune of one who has wronged me.

When I have done or said what is wrong, may I never wait for the rebuke of others, but always rebuke myself until I make amends.... May I win no victory that harms either me or my opponent.... May I reconcile friends who are angry with one another.

May I, to the extent of my power, give all needful help to my friends and to all who are in want. May I never fail a friend in danger.

When visiting those in grief, may I be able, by gentle and healing words, to soften their pain.... May I respect myself.... May I always tame that which rages within me....

May I accustom myself to be gentle and never be angry with people because of circumstances.

May I never discuss who is wicked and what wicked things he has done, but know good men and follow in their footsteps, through Christ Our Lord. Amen.

A Universal Prayer
(composed by Pope Clement XI)

O my God, I believe in Thee; do Thou strengthen my faith. All my hopes are in Thee; do Thou secure them. I love Thee with my whole heart; teach me to love Thee daily more and more. I am sorry that I have offended Thee; do Thou increase my sorrow.

I adore Thee as my first beginning; I aspire after Thee as my last end. I give Thee thanks as my constant benefactor; I call upon Thee as my sovereign protector.

Vouchsafe, O my God, to conduct me by Thy wisdom, to restrain me by Thy justice, to comfort me by Thy mercy, to defend me by Thy power.

To Thee I desire to consecrate all my thoughts, words, actions, and sufferings; that henceforward I may think of Thee, speak of Thee, constantly refer all my actions to Thy greater glory, and suffer willingly whatever Thou shall appoint.

Lord, I desire in all things that Thy will may be done, because it is Thy will, in the manner Thou willest, and for as long as willest.

I beg of Thee to enlighten my understanding, to inflame my will, to purify my body, and to sanctify my soul.

Grant that I be not puffed up with pride, moved by flattery, deceived by the world, or duped by the devil.

Give me grace to purify my memory, to bridle my tongue, to restrain my eyes, and to mortify my senses.

Give me strength, O my God, to expiate my offenses, to overcome my temptations, to subdue my passions, and to acquire the virtues proper for my state.

Fill my heart with a tender affection for Thy goodness, a hatred for my faults, a love for my neighbor, and a contempt for the world.

Let me always remember to be submissive to my superiors, patient with my inferiors, faithful to my friends, and charitable to my enemies.

Grant, O Jesus, that I may remember Thy precept and example by loving my enemies, bearing with injuries, doing good to those who persecute me, and praying for those who slander me.

Assist me to overcome sensuality by mortification, avarice by almsdeeds, anger by meekness, and tepidity by devotion.

O my God, make me prudent in my undertakings, courageous in dangers, patient in afflictions, and humble in prosperity.

Grant that I may be ever attentive in my prayers, temperate at meals, diligent in employments, and constant in good resolutions.

Let my conscience be ever upright and pure, my exterior modest, my conversation edifying, and my life according to rule.

Assist me, that I may continually labor to overcome nature, to correspond with Thy grace, to keep Thy commandments, and to work out my salvation.

Help me to obtain holiness of life by a sincere confession of my sins, by a devout reception of the Body of Christ, by a continual recollection of mind, and by a pure intention of heart.

Reveal to me, O my God, the nothingness of this world, the greatness of heaven, the shortness of time, and the length of eternity.

Grant that I may prepare for death, that I may fear Thy judgments, that I may escape hell and, in the end, obtain heaven, through the merits of Our Lord Jesus Christ.

Prayer of St. Ignatius

Take, O Lord, and receive my entire liberty, my memory, my understanding, and my whole will. All that I am, all that I have, Thou hast given me, and I will give it back again to Thee to be disposed of according to Thy good pleasure. Give me only Thy love and Thy grace; with Thee, I am rich enough, nor do I ask for aught besides. Amen.

A Prayer of the Church under Grievous Persecutions

Thou hast broken up the fountains and the torrents; thou hast dried up the Ethan rivers.

Thine is the day, and thine is the night; thou hast made the morning light and the sun.

Thou hast made all the borders of the earth; the summer and the spring were formed by thee.

Remember this, the enemy hath reproached the Lord; and a foolish people hath provoked thy name.

Deliver not up to beasts the souls that confess to thee, and forget not to the end the souls of thy poor.

Have regard to thy covenant, for they that are the obscure of the earth have been filled with dwellings of iniquity.

Let not the humble be turned away with confusion; the poor and needy shall praise thy name.

Arise, O God, judge thy own cause: remember thy reproaches with which the foolish man hath reproached thee all the day.

Forget not the voices of thy enemies—the pride of them that hate thee ascendeth continually. (Ps. 73 [74]:15–23)

LORD, TEACH US TO PRAY

A Prayer of a Sinner, Trusting in the Mercies of God

Out of the depths, I have cried to thee, O Lord: Lord, hear my voice.

Let thy ears be attentive to the voice of my supplication.

If thou, O Lord, wilt make iniquities: Lord, who shall stand it? For with thee there is merciful forgiveness: and by reason of thy law, I have waited for thee, O Lord.

My soul hath relied on his word: my soul hath hoped in the Lord.

From the morning watch even unto night, let Israel hope in the Lord. Because with the Lord, there is mercy: and with him plentiful redemption. And he shall redeem Israel from all his iniquities. (Ps. 129 [130])

Prayer before a Crucifix

Behold, O kind and most sweet Jesus, I cast myself upon my knees in Thy sight, and with the most fervent desire of my soul I pray and beseech Thee that Thou wouldst impress upon my heart lively sentiments of faith, hope, and charity, with true repentance for my sins, and a firm desire of amendment, whilst with deep affection and grief of soul I ponder within myself and mentally contemplate Thy five most precious wounds; having before my eyes that which David in prophecy made Thee say concerning Thyself, O good Jesus: "They have pierced my hands and feet; they have numbered all my bones."

An Exhortation to the Praise and Service of God

I will bless the Lord at all times: his praises shall be always in my mouth. In the Lord shall my soul be praised: let the meek hear and rejoice. Oh, magnify the Lord with me; and let us extol his name together.

I sought the Lord, and he heard me, and he delivered me from all my troubles.

Come ye to him and be enlightened, and your faces shall not be confounded.

This poor man cried, and the Lord heard him and saved him out of all his troubles.

The angel of the Lord shall encamp round about them that fear him and shall deliver them.

Oh, taste, and see that the Lord is sweet: blessed is the man that hopeth in him.

Fear the Lord, all ye his saints, for there is no want to them that fear him.

The rich have wanted and have suffered hunger, but they that see the Lord shall not be deprived of any good.

Come, children, hearken to me: I will teach you the fear of the Lord. Who is the man that desireth life, who loveth to see good days? Keep thy tongue from evil and thy lips from speaking guile. Turn away from evil and do good; seek after peace and pursue it.

The eyes of the Lord are upon the just and his ears unto their prayers. But the countenance of the Lord is against them that do evil things, to cut off the remembrance of them from the earth.

The just cried, and the Lord heard them and delivered them out of all their troubles. The Lord is nigh unto them that are of a contrite heart; and he will save the humble of spirit.

Many are the afflictions of the just, but out of them all will the Lord deliver them. The Lord keepeth all their bones, not one of them shall be broken.

The death of the wicked is very evil, and they that hate the just shall be guilty. The Lord will redeem the souls of his servants: and none of them that trust in him shall offend. (Ps. 33 [34])

An Exhortation to Despise This World
and the Short Prosperity of the Wicked
and to Trust in Providence

Trust in the Lord, and do good, and dwell in the land, and thou shalt be fed with its riches.

Delight in the Lord and he will give thee the requests of thy heart. Commit thy way to the Lord, and trust in him, and he will do it. And he will bring forth thy justice as the light, and thy judgment as the noonday. Be subject to the Lord and pray to him.

Envy, not the man who prospereth in his way; the man who doth unjust things....

The wicked have drawn out the sword, they have bent their bow, to cast down the poor and needy, to kill the upright of heart. Let their sword enter into their own hearts, and let their bow be broken....

Decline from evil and do good, and dwell forever and ever.

For the Lord loveth judgment and will not forsake his saints; they shall be preserved forever.

The unjust shall be punished, and the seed of the wicked shall perish. But the just shall inherit the land, and shall dwell therein for evermore. (Ps. 36 [37]:3–7, 14, 15, 27–29)

"To Our Lady"

Lovely Lady dressed in blue.
Teach me how to pray!
God was just your little Boy,
Tell me what to say!

Did you lift Him up sometimes,
Gently, on your knee?
Did you sing to Him the way
Mother does to me?

Did you hold His hand at night?
Did you ever try
Telling stories of the world?
Oh! And did He cry?

Do you really think He cares
If I tell Him things —
Little things that happen?
And do the angels' wings

Make a noise? And can He hear
Me if I speak low?
Does He understand me now?
Tell me — for you know.

Lovely Lady dressed in blue,
Teach me how to pray!
God was just your little Boy,
And you know the way.

(Mary Dixon Thayer)

Acknowledgments

I want to thank Almighty God for the health of mind, body, and spirit to put together these reflections.

To my good wife, Isabel, my children, and my grandchildren, who keep me young at heart and are truly a blessing from God. Thank you for sharing in my joy.

I wish to express my gratitude to members of the Archbishop Fulton John Sheen Foundation in Peoria, Illinois—in particular, to the Most Rev. Daniel R. Jenky, C.S.C., bishop of Peoria, for his leadership and fidelity to the cause of Sheen's canonization and to the creation of this book.

To Julie Enzenberger, O.C.V., who repeated to me time and time again Sheen's words: "Believe the incredible, and you can do the impossible."

To Sr. Connie Derby, R.S.M., director of archives and records at the Diocese of Rochester, for all her help in assisting me to source many of the original publications of Archbishop Fulton J. Sheen's works.

To the parish priest of my youth, Father Alfred (Bud) Quesnelle (1921–2010, R.I.P.), who, when I was just seven, demonstrated to me what it is to have amazement and awe before the Eucharistic Heart of Jesus. His lessons of "seeking the Lord where He may be found," especially in the tabernacle, have guided my spiritual life.

To my parents, John and Maxine Smith, who, on the day of my Baptism, entrusted me to the care of the Sacred Heart of Jesus and the

Immaculate Heart of Mary. This one act of love made many years ago has indelibly marked my life. I am eternally grateful for this consecration.

I am also grateful for my parents' example of love for the Most Holy Eucharist, by attending Mass daily. The Eucharist truly was the source and summit of their lives. My father would remind me to "give your employer a good forty hours of work each week, and never forget to give the Lord a good forty-hour devotion from time to time."

To the tens of thousands of people I have met in my travels, giving presentations about Archbishop Fulton J. Sheen at parishes, conferences, universities, high schools, church groups, and even pubs: thank you for sharing with me your many "Sheen Stories." I truly cherish each and every one of them.

And lastly, to Archbishop Fulton J. Sheen, whose teachings on Our Lord's Passion and His Seven Last Words continue to inspire me to love God more and to appreciate the gift of the Church. His teachings and his encouragement to make a Holy Hour each day have been a true gift in my life. May I be so blessed as to imitate Archbishop Sheen's love for the saints, the sacraments, the Eucharist, and the Mother of God. May the Good Lord grant him a very high place in heaven!

—Al Smith

Fulton J. Sheen

(1895–1979)

Fulton John Sheen was born in El Paso, Illinois, in 1895. In high school, he won a three-year university scholarship, but he turned it down to pursue a vocation to the priesthood. He attended St. Viator College Seminary in Illinois and St. Paul Seminary in Minnesota. In 1919, he was ordained a priest for the Diocese of Peoria, Illinois. He earned a licentiate in sacred theology and a bachelor of canon law at the Catholic University of America and a doctorate at the Catholic University of Louvain, Belgium.

Sheen received numerous teaching offers but declined them in obedience to his bishop and became an assistant pastor in a rural parish. Having thus tested his obedience, the bishop later permitted him to teach at the Catholic University of America and at St. Edmund's College in Ware, England, where he met G.K. Chesterton, whose weekly BBC radio broadcast inspired Sheen's later NBC broadcast, *The Catholic Hour* (1930–1952).

In 1952, Sheen began appearing on ABC in his own series, *Life Is Worth Living*. Despite being given a time slot that forced him to compete with Milton Berle and Frank Sinatra, the dynamic Sheen enjoyed enormous success and in 1954 reach tens of millions of viewers, non-Catholics as well as Catholics.

When asked by Pope Pius XII how many converts he had made, Sheen responded, "Your Holiness, I have never counted them. I am always afraid if I did count them, I might think I made them, instead of the Lord." Sheen gave annual Good Friday homilies at New York's St. Patrick's Cathedral, led numerous retreats for priests and religious, and preached at summer conferences in England.

"If you want people to stay as they are," he said, "tell them what they want to hear. If you want to improve them, tell them what they should know." This he did, not only in his preaching but also in the more than ninety books he wrote. His *Peace of Soul* was sixth on the *New York Times* best-seller list.

Sheen served as auxiliary bishop of New York (1951–1966) and as bishop of Rochester (1966–1969).

His two great loves were for the Blessed Mother and the Eucharist. He made a daily Holy Hour before the Blessed Sacrament, from which he drew strength and inspiration to preach the gospel and in the presence of which he prepared his homilies. "I beg [Christ] every day to keep me strong physically and alert mentally in order to preach His gospel and proclaim His Cross and Resurrection," he said. "I am so happy doing this that I sometimes feel that when I come to the good Lord in Heaven, I will take a few days' rest and then ask Him to allow me to come back again to this earth to do some more work."

The good Lord called Fulton Sheen home in 1979. His television broadcasts, now on tape, and his books continue his earthly work of winning souls for Christ. Sheen's cause for canonization was opened in 2002. In 2012, Pope Benedict XVI declared him "Venerable." (The rest is in God's hands.)

Fulton J. Sheen Works Used in This Book

The Armor of God: Reflections and Prayers for Wartime. New York: P. J. Kenedy and Sons, 1943.

Calvary and the Mass: A Missal Companion. New York: P. J. Kenedy and Sons, 1936.

The Holy Hour: Reading and Prayers for a Daily Hour of Meditation. Prepared for the National Council of Catholic Men. Huntington, IN: Our Sunday Visitor, 1946.

The Priest Is Not His Own. New York: McGraw-Hill, 1963.

The Seven Last Words. Address delivered on Good Friday, 1935. Transcribed by and prepared for the National Council of Catholic Men. In *The Fullness of Christ*. Huntington, IN: Our Sunday Visitor, 1936.

Sophia Institute

Sophia Institute is a nonprofit institution that seeks to nurture the spiritual, moral, and cultural life of souls and to spread the Gospel of Christ in conformity with the authentic teachings of the Roman Catholic Church.

Sophia Institute Press fulfills this mission by offering translations, reprints, and new publications that afford readers a rich source of the enduring wisdom of mankind.

Sophia Institute also operates the popular online resource CatholicExchange.com. *Catholic Exchange* provides world news from a Catholic perspective as well as daily devotionals and articles that will help readers to grow in holiness and live a life consistent with the teachings of the Church.

In 2013, Sophia Institute launched Sophia Institute for Teachers to renew and rebuild Catholic culture through service to Catholic education. With the goal of nurturing the spiritual, moral, and cultural life of souls, and an abiding respect for the role and work of teachers, we strive to provide materials and programs that are at once enlightening to the mind and ennobling to the heart; faithful and complete, as well as useful and practical.

Sophia Institute gratefully recognizes the Solidarity Association for preserving and encouraging the growth of our apostolate over the course of many years. Without their generous and timely support, this book would not be in your hands.

www.SophiaInstitute.com
www.CatholicExchange.com
www.SophiaInstituteforTeachers.org

Sophia Institute Press® is a registered trademark of Sophia Institute.
Sophia Institute is a tax-exempt institution as defined by the
Internal Revenue Code, Section 501(c)(3). Tax ID 22-2548708.